Doctrine & Theology

INVITED TO GO AND TEACH

Student Workbook

Doctrine & Apologetics
Student Workbook

© 2012
Published by Wheaton Press
Wheaton, Illinois

www.WheatonPress.com

ISBN-13:978-0615769684
ISBN-10: 0615769683

1. Christian Education – Discipleship 2. Spiritual Formation – Discipleship. 3. Foundations of Faith – Education. 4. Nonfiction-Religion and Spirituality-Christian Life. 5. Nonfiction-Spiritual Growth-Christ-centered.

Copyright and Trademark Standard

Contact the publisher for discounted copies for partner schools and receive free resources and training for teachers. Learn more at WheatonPress.com or email WheatonPress@gmail.com

FOR OUR STUDENTS AND THOSE THEY WILL INFLUENCE

WATCH YOUR LIFE AND
DOCTRINE

I Timothy 4:16, NIV

Doctrine & Apologetics

INVITED TO GO AND TEACH

Equipping Students to Reflect Christ

	YEAR ONE	YEAR TWO	YEAR THREE	YEAR FOUR
Growth Emphasis	An Emphasis on Believing	An Emphasis on Following	An Emphasis on Loving	An Emphasis on Going
Essential Questions	1. What does a healthy, mature follower of Christ believe? 2. How does a healthy, mature follower of Christ live?	3. How do I grow as a healthy, mature follower of Christ? 4. How do I equip others to grow as healthy, mature followers of Christ?	5. Who do others say Jesus is? 6. Who do I say Jesus is?	7. What do I believe? 8. Why do I believe? 9. How will I communicate to others?
Essential Outcomes	Understand and articulate Christ-centered **beliefs**	Develop authentic Christ-centered **values**	Develop and articulate a Christ-centered **vision**	Develop a clear Christ-centered personal **mission**
Courses	Foundations of Faith	Spiritual Formations Leadership, Evangelism, & Discipleship	Life of Christ Philosophy & Theology	Doctrine & Apologetics Christ & Culture

DOCTRINE & APOLOGETICS

Equipping students to reflect Christ in their circles of influence.

Syllabus   6

Unit 1 Prolegomena   15

Unit 2 Revelation   53

Unit 3 Bibliology   61

Unit 4 Theology Proper   67

Unit 5 Christology   73

Unit 6 Pneumatology   79

Unit 7 Anthropology   103

Unit 8 Soteriology   109

Unit 9 Angelology   120

Unit 10 Ecclesiology   126

Unit 11 Eschatology   132

Unit 12 Applied Theology   152

DOCTRINE & APOLOGETICS

Equipping students to reflect Christ in their circles of influence.

Course description

This course is designed to equip the Christian with answers to the most difficult questions posed by both believers and unbelievers. Within the theological framework, students will study major doctrines pertaining to the existence and nature of God, evil, the nature of man, Scripture as the source of truth, and the church as the body of Christ. Students will understand and apply those doctrines in the context of living out one's faith in a contemporary culture of competing worldviews and relativism.

General outcomes

A. Students will interact within the context of community to exercise critical theological thinking and gain an appreciation for the significance of theology in the application of their personal worldview.

B. Students will develop and articulate a personal doctrine statement.

C. Students will develop and articulate a personal apologetic.

Essential outcomes

1. What do I believe?

2. Why do I believe it?

3. What difference will my beliefs make in my life?

Text

Little, Paul E. *Know What You Believe.* Downers Grove, IL: InterVarsity Press, 2008.

Little, Paul E. *Know Why You Believe.* Downers Grove, IL: InterVarsity Press, 2008.

Student-supplied Bible

Key learning goals to know and understand

a. You will learn to anticipate and trust in the power of God's truth to change your life (prolegomena).

b. You will deepen your confidence in God's personal and intentional desire to be known through general and specific revelation.

c. You will deepen (or form) your conviction that the Bible, as God's Word, can be trusted more than feelings, values, opinions, and culture (bibliology).

d. You will deepen (or form) a deeper sense of the Trinity's role in your salvation and sanctification (theology proper).

e. You will develop an understanding of Jesus' nature as both God and man that will protect you against false teaching and deepen your confidence and trust in Christ (Christology).

f. You will experience a new sense of security in your relationship with God based on the presence of the Holy Spirit in your life (pneumatology).

g. You will deepen your appreciation for worshiping God as creator (anthropology).

h. You will wrestle with the arguments, implications, and applications of monergistic and synergistic theological frameworks (soteriology).

i. You will develop an appreciation for your relationship to angels, demons, and Satan within the framework of God's eternal plan (angelology).

j. You will deepen your love and commitment to Christ's body, the church (ecclesiology).

k. You will see the Second Coming through the lens of hope and purpose (eschatology).

l. You will develop a personal growth plan for next steps after high school (discipleship).

Key Skills

Students will utilize and refine tools such as writing, studying, thinking, discussing, presenting, and communicating theologically, which will help them develop competence and confidence in articulating a distinctly Christ-centered worldview through a theological and biblical lens.

Reading Assignments

	Unit	Text and Chapter(s):
Unit One:	Prolegomena	Know Why You Believe, 1
Unit Two:	Revelation	Know Why You Believe, 5, 9 Know What You Believe, 1
Unit Three:	Bibliology	Know Why You Believe, 6-7 Know What You Believe, 1
Unit Four:	Theology Proper	Know Why You Believe, 2 Know What You Believe, 2
Unit Five:	Christology	Know Why You Believe, 3-4 Know What You Believe, 3-4
Unit Six:	Pneumatology	Know What You Believe, 6
Unit Seven:	Anthropology	Know What You Believe, 5
Unit Eight:	Soteriology	Know Why You Believe, 8 Know What You Believe, 7
Unit Nine:	Angelology	Know What You Believe, 8
Unit Ten:	Ecclesiology	Know What You Believe, 9
Unit Eleven:	Eschatology	Know What You Believe, 10
Unit Twelve:	Applied Theology	Know Why You Believe, 11-12

Assessment of learning

There are three primary types of assessments you will participate in during this class:

Formative assessments: These are your first drafts of your position papers. They are non-graded and demonstrate your learning progression and process.

Summative assessments: These are your final drafts of your position papers. They are the graded demonstrations of what you have learned. [Note: at any point in the semester, your last copy (or highest grade) of a position paper becomes your summative assessment for that doctrine.]

Student-initiated assessment: This demonstration of higher learning is initiated at any time during the semester by a student who resubmits a formative position paper to demonstrate a higher level of learning in the area of a particular essential question. This ensures that throughout the semester, learning is the constant and time is the variable.

Summative assessments:

For every learning objective, you will be assessed via a doctrinal position paper on what you "Know, Understand, and Do" (KUD) as a result of your interaction with the material.

Each position paper will assess three areas of learning through *What, Why,* and *So What* sections in your paper.

1. **What:** Doctrinal understanding. This section is a demonstration of what you *know* to be true. (40%)

2. **Why:** Doctrinal apologetic. This section is a demonstration of your *understanding* of the reason you believe (1 Pet. 3:15). (40%)

3. **So What:** Practical application. This section is a demonstration of what you will *do* to apply your knowledge and understanding to your life beyond the classroom. (20%)

Position Paper Proficiency Scale

Learning objectives in the *What* and *Why* sections of the paper will be based on the following scale of proficiency.

0	1	2	3	4
Not attempted.	Demonstrates little, if any, knowledge or understanding of material explicitly taught in class. Zero to 50 percent of statements are backed up by outside references.	Demonstrates basic knowledge or understanding of material explicitly taught in class. Fifty percent of statements are backed up by references.	Demonstrates knowledge or understanding of material explicitly taught in class and includes material explicitly taught in the course textbook. Seventy-five percent of statements are backed up by references.	Demonstrates Level 3 knowledge and understanding and includes material pulled from additional outside academic/theological resources, or demonstrates higher-level critical thinking by connecting specific doctrines to other essential learning outcomes, essential questions, or doctrines. Ninety-one to one hundred percent of statements are backed up by outside references and sources.

Learning objectives in the *So What* section of the paper will be based on the following scale of proficiency.

0	1	2
Not attempted.	Student demonstrates a generic or simplistic application. Sentences or thoughts are not complete or do not meet the minimum of four sentences for a complete paragraph. Student demonstrates basic, if any, interaction with the material in a personal way. Thoughts are generic or incomplete in nature.	Evidence is given that the student interacted with the significance of his or her beliefs in a meaningful way. References are made to how the student's beliefs or apologetic impact his or her life and demonstrate higher-level thought, critical thinking, and personal reflection. Thoughts are complete and demonstrate an interaction with the material in a minimum of a four-sentence paragraph.

Assessment of learning

Position Papers	Date due	Proficiency: *Know/What* section	Proficiency: *Understand/ Why* section	Proficiency: *Do/So What* Section	Total %
1 Peter 3:15 reflection paper					
Bibliology					
Theology proper					
Christology					
Pneumatology					
Appendix paper					
Anthropology					
Soteriology					
Angelology					
Ecclesiology					
Eschatology					
Presentation/ Reflection paper					

Doctrine & Apologetics
Essential questions

Weekend Reading	Monday	Tuesday	Block day	Friday
Prolegomena		What is the learning goal for this class? Am I prepared to meet the challenge Beyond the Walls?	What is the challenge of I Peter 3:15? Am I prepared to meet the challenge of a communicating a reasoned faith? How will this class support me to meet the challenges ahead?	YouTube Friday How does worldview impact doctrine & belief? Does Satan exist?
Doctrine & Apologetics. *Know Why You Believe* I	How does the world challenge my faith?	How do I face the fear of doubt?	How do metaphysics, epistemology, knowledge and doctrine intersect with doctrine?	YouTube Friday How do we have Theological conversations?
Revelation *Know Why You Believe* 5, 9 *Know What You Believe* I	I Peter Quiz Theological Conflict part I	Theological Conflict part 2	What are my personal goals for this class? What are our shared goals for this class?	YouTube Friday Does science silence God?
	Paper I due What is general revelation?	Does God really hold people accountable through General Revelation?	Can evolution be trusted? Can Genesis be trusted?	How do I write a Theological Position Paper?
Bibliology *Know Why You Believe* 6-7 *Know What You Believe* I	How do I write a personal doctrinal statement? How do I write a personal apologetic?	How do I communicate what I believe?	Is the Biblical Text trustworthy?	Are the Biblical documents reliable?
	Revelation paper due Does Archeology verify Scripture?	What is textual criticism?	Can I trust the Bible?	YouTube Friday Does God exist?

Doctrine & Apologetics
Essential questions

Unit and reading	Monday	Tuesday	Block day	Friday
Theology Proper *Know Why You Believe* 2 *Know What You Believe* 2	Bibliology paper due What is Theology Proper?	Theology Proper Mini-Projects	Mini-Project Presentations	YouTube Friday Is the resurrection real?
Christology I *Know Why You Believe* 3-4 *Know What You Believe* 3-4	Theology proper paper due Is Christ God? Dies Christ claim to be God?	Christology Mini-Project	Christology Mini-Project	Why is it important to know that the Holy Spirit is a personality? What is the practical role of the Holy Spirit in the Trinity?
Pneumatology Know What You Believe 6	Christology Paper due When are we sealed, indwelt, and baptized by the Holy Spirit? How did Christ relate to the Holy Spirit?	What does the Bible really say about the Holy Spirit? I Corinthians Project	What does the Bible really say about the Holy Spirit? I Corinthians Project	Pneumatology FAQs & Workday
Anthropology Know What You Believe 5	What am I learning? How is it relevant?	What is the doctrine of Theological Anthropology? Mini-Projects Research	Mini-projects Presentations	What are some of the contemporary doctrinal issues within soteriology? What are the various views of the atonement?
Soteriology *Know What You Believe* 7 *Know Why You Believe* 8	Anthropology paper due What are the elements of saving faith? What are the results of saving faith?	Research results, Socratic community Did God choose us?	Is there an age of accountability? What is sanctification, and how does God change us?	YouTube Friday Are angels and demons real?

Doctrine & Apologetics
Essential questions

Unit and reading	Monday	Tuesday	Block Day	Friday
Angelology Know What You Believe 8	Soteriology paper due How do we separate fact from fiction when it comes to angels, demons and Satan?	How do we separate fact from fiction when it comes to angels, demons and Satan?	How do we separate fact from fiction when it comes to angels, demons and Satan?	What is the current state of the church?
Ecclesiology *Know What You Believe* 9	Angelology paper due What is God's vision for the church?	What is God's vision for the church?	Who qualifies for church leadership?	Is Eschatology relevant?
Eschatology *Know What You Believe* 10	Angelology paper due What do Christians believe about the end times?	What do Christians believe about the end times?	How does Eschatology lead us to applied Theology?	Reading Day
Applied doctrine *Know Why You Believe* 11-12	Eschatology Paper Due Does Christianity differ from other world religions? Is the Christian experience valid?	Did I achieve the desired outcome of Doctrine & Apologetics? Am I prepared to meet the challenge beyond the walls?	Work Day	Work Day
	Summative oral and written presentations	Summative oral and written presentations	Summative oral and written presentations	Final Assessment

Prolegomena

Doctrine & Apologetics

INVITED TO GO AND TEACH

Unit Essential Questions

1. What is doctrine and theology?

2. Why do doctrine and theology matter?

Unit Learning Objectives

A   To understand the essential questions, learning objectives, and expectations for this class

B   To identify my personal learning needs

C   To develop a personalized learning plan for this class

D   To understand the reason for doctrine and theology

Unit Learning Assessments

"Expectations for growth" personal reflection handout

The global student assessment

Final exam pre-assessment

Personal spiritual formation assessment

Daily Essential Questions

1. What is the learning goal for doctrine and apologetics?

2. What is the challenge of 1 Peter 3:15?

3. How does worldview impact doctrine?

4. How does the world challenge my faith?

5. How do I face the fear of doubt?

6. How do metaphysics, epistemology, knowledge and doctrine intersect?

7. How do I apply the discipline of metaphysics and epistemology to a theological conversation?

8. How do I deal with conflict?

9. How do I deal with conflict? (part 2)

10. What are my goals for this class?

Engage your mind = satisfying comprehension

The key concept in the idea of "reasoned faith" is that of satisfying comprehension.

One of the goals for the *Foundations* class is that you will have the opportunity to build a satisfying comprehension of your faith in a world that will attack your faith and your beliefs.

A strong foundation for faith will engage your mind and will give you something to "rest" your faith in during the storms of life.

If we do not engage your minds, then faith becomes flimsy and overly emotional.

The result is we end up "blown about by every wind of new teaching" (Eph. 4:14, NLT) or doctrine, or our foundation fails us in the midst of life's challenges.

But weak, unreasoned faith is not the type of faith Jesus expects of his followers.

Rather, we are invited to love the Lord with all of our mind.

Why would we love the Lord with all of our minds in an AP math or science class, but be satisfied with only a Sunday school Bible lesson?

As you take this course, you will be invited to engage in difficult thinking and to "dig deep."

Your faith will be challenged in this course, but the goal is that it will come out stronger as a result.

So what will it take for us to engage our minds and reach satisfying comprehension as a community?

Reflection and response

1. What can I expect from this class?

2. What can I expect from my teacher?

3. What do I need to expect from my peers?

4. What do I need to expect from myself?

Pre-assessment

Name: _____   Period: _____

1. Write out 1 Peter 3:15 from memory.

Define the following theological terms. Use Scripture to support your answers.

2. Inspiration:

3. Inerrancy:

4. Special revelation:

5. General revelation:

6. Textual criticism:

7. Anthropology:

8. Trinity:

9. Kenosis:

10. Incarnation:

11. Hypostatic Union:

Pre-assessment

12. Penal substitutionary atonement:

13. Theophany:

14. Christophany:

15. Atonement:

16. Appeasement:

17. Ransom:

18. Substitution:

19. Reconciliation:

20. Total depravity:

21. Election:

22. Predestination:

23. Foreknowledge:

24. Monergism:

25. Synergism:

19

Pre-assessment

26. Tribulation:

27. Rapture:

28. Pretribulation:

29. Midtribulation:

30. Amillennial:

31. Judgment seat of Christ:

32. Judgment of the sheep and the goats:

33. Revelation:

34. Bibliology:

35. Pneumatology:

36. Ecclesiology:

37. Eschatology:

Pre-assessment

Short answer: Use Scripture references to back up each of your answers.

1. What is your view on evolution and creationism? What is your apologetic for your belief?

2. What is the name of the argument for God's existence based on the law of cause and effect?

3. What is the difference between God's directive will and His permissive will? What biblical passages support your explanation?

4. Many people claim Jesus was a great moral teacher, but He was not the Son of God. How would you respond to such a person? Use Scripture to back up your response.

5. Read Matthew 28:11-15. According to this passage, even the enemies of Christ admitted His tomb was empty. The truth of Christ's resurrection rests on how the tomb was emptied. The authorities claimed Jesus' followers removed the body. Other explanations are often given, as well: that the authorities moved the body or the disciples returned to the wrong tomb. What makes these explanations reasonable or unreasonable? Back up your position.

Pre-assessment

1. List and explain four ways Jesus proved He is fully God. Use Scripture to back up your response.

    1.

    2.

    3.

    4.

2. How do we know that Jesus was fully human in addition to being fully God? Why does it matter? Use Scripture to back up your response.

3. What are three reasons Jesus had to live a perfect life?

    1.

    2.

    3.

4. Now that Jesus has ascended into heaven, what role does He assume? Use Scripture to back up your response.

5. How did Christ's death fulfill the Old Testament sacrificial system? Use Scripture to back up your response.

Pre-assessment

6. How would you answer a friend who asked you, "How could one person die to save the whole world?" What Scriptures would you use to defend your answer?

7. Why is it important to know the Holy Spirit is a personality? Use Scripture to defend your answer.

8. List and explain five aspects of the Holy Spirit's work in the Old Testament. What Scripture would you use to support your answers?

   1.

   2.

   3.

   4.

   5.

9. Explain this statement: "In the Old Testament, the Holy Spirit came on individuals temporarily."

Pre-assessment

10. Describe the New Testament arrival of the Holy Spirit. How does this compare to the arrival of the Holy Spirit in the Old Testament? What was God's purpose for the difference?

11. When are we sealed, indwelt, and baptized by the Holy Spirit?

12. How can you tell the difference between biblical miracles and "pagan" miracles?

13. Explain the meaning of the word "repentance" in practical terms.

14. What are the elements of saving faith?

15. What are the results of saving faith? Use Scripture to back up your answer.

16. List three facets of angelic activity. What verses support your position?

    1.

    2.

    3.

Pre-assessment

17. List four biblical truths about Satan. What verses support your position?

    1.

    2.

    3.

    4.

18. How does the word *ekklesia* describe the church?

19. Define the difference between premillennialism and amillennialism. Which one do you believe? Why? Defend your answer with Scripture.

20. Describe the three end-times judgments. What are the differences and significances of each?

21. How would you effectively answer a person who thinks your Christian experience is a fantasy? (1 Peter 3:15)

Pre-assessment

Life application essay

1. Two friends from school—a male and female—approach you in confidence and share with you that they have been sexually active together. As a result, she is pregnant and considering an abortion. How would you counsel her, and why? Use Scripture to back up your answer, however, you cannot use "thou shalt not kill."

   I would tell the couple that everything will work out and that you should be calm and peaceful in their journey.

Life application essay

2. Two nice young men come to your door. They are both wearing white shirts, black pants, and ties. You see their bicycles parked alongside the curb. Their nametags say their names are Elder Smith and Elder Jones. They would like to come in and "do a Bible study" with you.

   a. Under what circumstances would you invite them in?
   b. What items of spiritual warfare should you be particularly aware of?
   c. What ground rules should you set as a result?
   d. Outline their argument about Christ.
   e. What Scripture would you use as your apologetic to their claims?

   a. under no circumstances.
   b.

Pre-assessment

Life application essay

3. Your friend at work is a Jehovah's Witness. One day, while you are talking over lunch, he explains to you his belief that Jesus never actually claimed to be God. In fact, he pulls out his version of the Bible and shows you that in John 1, his Bible says Jesus was simply "a" god. What is your response? What argument would you use from the text to show how and why his version is a blatant mistranslation of Scripture? What verses would you reference to show how Christ claimed to be God in a way that even His enemies clearly understood His claim?

Every translation of the Bible says that
Jesus is

Life application essay

4. Two friends have a baby who dies tragically. You go to the hospital to visit them, and through their tears, one of them confesses to you that they don't know how this tragedy could have happened when they both have loved God their whole lives and kept themselves pure prior to marriage. Now they feel like God has turned His back on them, and they wonder whether they will see their baby in heaven. How would you use Scripture to counsel them?

I would

Pre-assessment

Life application essay

5. After leaving school, you start attending college and begin the process of looking for churches. One of the first churches you begin to attend seems like it would be a good fit. The people are nice, the worship is great, and the pastor seems like a cool guy. You begin talking with some of the people and asking questions about the church, and it casually slips out that the church believes the Bible "contains the Word of God." Is that a problem? Why or why not? Back up your response with Scripture.

    Yes, because it's claiming that the Bible has parts of the words of God rather than saying that the Bible is the word of God.

Life application essay

6. Marijuana is now legal in many different places around the world. Adherence to Romans 12 is no longer an issue: so should a Christian choose to smoke marijuana? Why or why not? Use Scripture as your apologetic for your answer.

What is the challenge of 1 Peter 3:15?

Am I prepared to meet the challenge beyond the walls?

But in your hearts revere Christ as Lord. Always be prepared to give an answer to everyone who asks you to give the reason for the hope that you have. But do this with gentleness and respect."

1 Peter 3:15, NIV

"Be diligent in these matters; give yourself wholly to them, so that everyone may see your progress. Watch your life and doctrine closely. Persevere in them, because if you do, you will save both yourself and your hearers."

1 Timothy 4:15-16, NIV

"You, however, must teach what is appropriate to sound doctrine. Teach the older men to be temperate, worthy of respect, self-controlled, and sound in faith, in love and in endurance. Likewise, teach the older women to be reverent in the way they live, not to be slanderers or addicted to much wine, but to teach what is good. Then they can urge the younger women to love their husbands and children, to be self-controlled and pure, to be busy at home, to be kind, and to be subject to their husbands, so that no one will malign the word of God. Similarly, encourage the young men to be self-controlled. In everything set them an example by doing what is good. In your teaching show integrity, seriousness and soundness of speech that cannot be condemned, so that those who oppose you may be ashamed because they have nothing bad to say about us."

Titus 2:1-8, NIV

"He must hold firmly to the trustworthy message as it has been taught, so that he can encourage others by sound doctrine and refute those who oppose it."

Titus 1:9, NIV

Self-assessment

In your own words, how would you describe the difference between faith and fantasy?

According to 1 Peter 3:15, what is "reasonable faith"?

How do you think this verse will apply to doctrine and theology?

Self-assessment

Where am I?

"But in your hearts revere Christ as Lord. Always be prepared to give an answer to everyone who asks you to give the reason for the hope that you have. But do this with gentleness and respect."

- 1 Peter 3:15, NIV

"Be diligent in these matters; give yourself wholly to them, so that everyone may see your progress. Watch your life and doctrine closely. Persevere in them, because if you do, you will save both yourself and your hearers."

- 1 Timothy 4:15-16, NIV

How will this class support me to meet the challenges ahead?
Why study doctrine?

"For the time will come when people will not put up with sound doctrine. Instead, to suit their own desires, they will gather around them a great number of teachers to say what their itching ears want to hear. They will turn their ears away from the truth and turn aside to myths."
- 2 Timothy 4:3-4, NIV

"Do not conform to the pattern of this world, but be transformed by the renewing of your mind. Then you will be able to test and approve what God's will is—his good, pleasing and perfect will."
- Romans 12:2, NIV

"So that you may become blameless and pure, 'children of God without fault in a crooked and depraved generation.' Then you will shine among them like stars in the sky as you hold firmly to the word of life."
- Philippians 2:15-16a, NIV

What is real?

How does worldview impact doctrine?

What are the two basic components of reality?

1.

2.

What are the basic views of reality?

1.

2.

3.

4.

5.

What are the seven core questions that probe the nature of reality?

1. What is real?
2. Who is God?
3. What is the basis of morality: right, wrong, and authority?
4. What is man?
5. What happens at death?
6. What is the meaning and purpose of human history?
7. Why are we here? Where are we going?

How does what we believe impact how we see the world?

YouTube Friday:
Does Satan Exist?

33

Know Why You Believe, Chapter 1

Chapter 1: Is Christianity rational?

Memorize 1 Peter 3:15.

- How do you feel the world challenges your faith? Give three specific examples.

- According to 1 Peter 3:15, we should "always be prepared to give an answer to everyone who asks you to give the reason for the hope that you have. But [we should] do this with gentleness and respect." How prepared are you to obey this command at this point in your life?

- What area do you need to work on this semester? (e.g., becoming more "prepared," becoming more secure in "the hope that you have," or answering with "gentleness and respect"?)

- Formulate a S.M.A.R.T. (Specific, Measurable, Achievable, Relevant, Time-Bound) goal for yourself as a commitment to what you want to get out of this course.

- How would obeying this verse help to dispel the faulty concept in some non-believers' minds that faith is "believing something you know isn't true"?

- It's worth following through on Peter's encouragement for us to be prepared to give an answer for the hope that is in us. So as you work your way through this book, take time to compile a list of reasons based on what you learn in each unit.

Know Why You Believe, Chapter 1

Chapter 1: Is Christianity rational?

35

What are the basic Christian doctrines?

Authentic = that which is true, real.

- Premise: Our daily thoughts, actions, and decisions are based on our conclusions of the nature of reality.

- Premise: If God is the originator of all things, then God is the original and authentic truth.

- Premise: All things are ultimately theological in nature.

- Premise: Systematic theology.

What are the basic Christian doctrines?

1. Revelation

2. Bibliology

3. Theology proper

4. Christology

5. Pneumatology

6. Anthropology

7. Soteriology

8. Angelology

9. Ecclesiology

10. Eschatology

Does Theological truth exist?

How do the disciplines of metaphysics, epistemology, and the concepts of knowledge and truth intersect?

"Until rather recent times Theology was considered the queen of the sciences and Systematic Theology the crown of the queen. But today the generality of so-called theological scholarship denies that it is a science and certainly the idea that it is the queen of the sciences."

- Henry C. Theissen,
- *Lectures in Systematic Theology*

What is doctrine?

Doctrine (Latin: *doctrina*) is a codification of beliefs or a body of taught principles, or positions believed to be true.

What is Christian doctrine?

What is apologetics?

What is Christian apologetics?

"See to it that no one takes you captive through hollow and deceptive philosophy, which depends on human tradition and the elemental spiritual forces of this world rather than on Christ."
Colossians 2:8, NIV

Does Theological truth exist?

How do the disciplines of metaphysics, epistemology, and the concepts of knowledge and truth intersect?

Premise: Sometimes the best we can do is get people to think about their own position.

1. What is the nature of God?

2. What is the nature of man?

3. What happens when we die?

Five critical questions

- Question 1.

- Question 2.

- Question 3.

- Question 4.

- Question 5.

Why is doctrine divisive?

Two reasons why there is conflict over doctrine.

1. People are conceited.

"We know that 'We all possess knowledge.' But knowledge puffs up while love builds up."
1 Corinthians 8:1b, NIV

"Do not let anyone who delights in false humility and the worship of angels disqualify you. Such a person also goes into great detail about what they have seen; they are puffed up with idle notions by their unspiritual mind."

Colossians 2:18, NIV

"If I have the gift of prophecy and can fathom all mysteries and all knowledge, and if I have a faith that can move mountains, but do not have love, I am nothing."

1 Corinthians 13:2, NIV

2. People are contenting.

"I felt compelled to write and urge you to contend for the faith that was once for all entrusted to God's holy people."
Jude 1:3, NIV

"Whatever happens, conduct yourselves in a manner worthy of the gospel of Christ. Then, whether I come and see you or only hear about you in my absence, I will know that you stand firm in the one Spirit, striving together as one for the faith of the gospel."

Philippians 1:27, NIV

"But there were also false prophets among the people, just as there will be false teachers among you. They will secretly introduce destructive heresies, even denying the sovereign Lord who bought them—bringing swift destruction on themselves."

2 Peter 2:1, NIV

What is the difference?

"But in your hearts revere Christ as Lord. Always be prepared to give an answer to everyone who asks you to give the reason for the hope that you have. But do this with gentleness and respect."
- 1 Peter 3:15, NIV

Conflict

Objectives:

- To identify and define two major types of conflict.
- To identify and learn tools to navigate types of negative and positive conflict.
- To identify the progressive stages of conflict and learn how to deescalate conflict.
- To identify and learn to apply effective conflict resolution techniques.

Perhaps the most widely participated in and yet least understood aspect of human communications is conflict and conflict resolution. Conflict is inevitable in human relations. Christ not only experienced conflict with those who desired to see His demise, but among those who were closest to Him as well.

- If conflict is enevitable then is it possible that there might be a difference between good conflict and bad conflict?

- If so, then how would we know the difference?

- If conflict is enevitable then should we fear conflict or embrace it?

Too often we fear conflict because we do not understand it and yet conflict has the potential to signify growth from infancy to maturity.

Ultimatly, everything in life is Theological and our personal perception of the world we share is based on our fundamental perspectives that are made up of our theological beliefs and positions whether we have ever taken the time to articulate them or not.

For some, previous baggage from the threat of conflict is enough to discourage us from the process of examining our beliefs. When this happens and we avoid conflict we risk missing the opportunity to grow up in our faith away from the spiritual infancy of unexamined beliefs toward spiritual maturity marked by examined, tested and reasoned faith (1 Peter 3:15).

The tragedy is that by protecting ourselves from the risk of conflict we expose ourselves to the risk of false teaching. Ephesians 4:14, Paul wrote;

> *"Then we will no longer be immature like children. We won't be tossed and blown about by every wind of new teaching. We will not be influenced when people try to trick us with lies so clever they sound like the truth. (NLT)*

Our overall goal for this course is to personalize our faith by examining what we believe; our reasons for why we believe it and to learn to communicate a reasoned faith with gentleness and respect.

For some, gentleness and respect would not typically be words to describe how we communicate. While others of us carry the mental, emotional and even physical scars of negative conflict and the thought of a conflict or a disagreement cues our emotions to shut down or to spring into action with an attempt to mediate peace before someone else gets hurt.

Whether we need to learn gentleness or we need to learn to find how not to allow the threat of conflict to control us the principles and understanding that you will gain through these next lessons will be valuable not only for this class but in any meaningful relationship.

The goal of these lessons is to equip us to not only share a common language as we face the potential opportunity for conflict but to share a set of common principles and process that will help us navigate our experience both in class and beyond the walls.

Types of Conflict

Internal vs. External Conflict

Internal conflict results between two or more people who are in direct relationship with one another and who are either on the same team or share the same mission or interest.

> The first recorded conflict recorded between Jesus and His disciples in the Gospel of Mark is an example of internal conflict (Mark 1:35-38). The disciples and Jesus are on the same team, but they are experience conflict over how to fulfill the mission of the group. The disciples observed Jesus casting out demons and healing many sick people, including Peters mother-in-law the evening before and believing they have the best interest of the group in mind, they want to Jesus to heal more people. It is not that they are intentionally attempting to work against Christ but having invested the morning in prayer with the Father, is not concerned about the desires of the crowd because He is focused on the mission of the Father.

External conflict can be defined as conflict resulting from secondary sources who oppose the mission of the individual or team.

> What separates internal conflict from external conflict is the interest or motivation of the parties involved.

> In the first twelve verses of Mark 2, it quickly becomes apparent that the scribes have neither the paralytic's interests nor the interests of this new rabbi and His disciples in mind when they begin to question Christ and His motives. Unlike the disciples they did not simply disagree about the best way to accomplish a shared mission they disagreed with the premise of the mission.

Respond

> Why is it important to identify the difference between internal and external conflict?

> How could this distinction equip you to view a current conflict in a different way?

Types of Conflict

Content vs. Relational Conflict

In addition to understanding the distinction between internal and external conflict in the context of disciplemaking relationships, it is also helpful to make the important distinction between content-centered conflict and relational conflict.

Content conflict can be defined as conflict that centers on objects, events, or persons that are external to the parties involved. Content conflict centers on objects, events, and persons that are external to the parties involved.

Relational conflict centers on the relationship between the two parties—who is in charge, the equality of the relationship, and who gets the final word.

What does this mean?

Internal content-centered conflict is healthy for a meaningful relationship. It is a strong indicator of trust and engagement within a relationship when both sides state opinions regarding the best way to accomplish a mission. This is what we see in the conflict between Christ and His disciples. They both want what they believe is best for the mission and the relationship but they disagree on the means.

Whereas external relational conflict is destructive. For example, in Mark 2, the external conflict coming from the scribes and religious leaders quickly deteriorates into relational-centered conflict.

It is dangerous when we view conflict through the lens of relationship, because then conflict becomes about attacking the other person and it quickly deteriorates into an us vs. them or a win-and-lose scenario.

The bottom line

Whether it is in a marriage relationship, a team, or a small group discipleship relationship or a class dialogue, it is crucial for healthy relationships to ensure that our conflict is content centered

Respond

Why is it important to identify the difference between content and relational conflict?

How could this distinction equip you to view a current conflict in a different way?

Types of Conflict

Conflict Stages	The stages of conflict in the life of Christ

Conflict Stages

1. Mild Difference

Communication is open and reasonably clear. However, if another party interferes at this point, it could cause a problem that was not there before.

2. Disagreement

Communication is guarded. Conditional comments are made. There are strong opinions on both sides and neither side is willing to budge.

3. Dispute

Communication is tense and limited. Sides are more polarized. Voices may be raised and unrelated issues are brought up. Conflict shows increasing signs of moving away from content and becoming relationally centered.

4. Campaigning or Litigation

Communication involves others who are unrelated to the original issue.

Attempts are made to sway people toward one side or another (similar to a political campaign). In Litigation, communication is blocked by legal action. At this point, communication has failed.

5. Fight and/or War

Communication is marked by violence or destructive behavior. Punches are thrown, bombs are dropped, and the relationship dies.

NOTE: Stages four and five can be interchangeable or done at the same time. Or, if resolution seems impossible, they are often skipped completely.

The stages of conflict in the life of Christ

1. Mild Difference

Mark 2:6-7

2. Disagreement

Mark 2:16-17

Mark 2:18-19, 24

3. Dispute

Mark 2:18-19, 24

4. Campaigning or Litigation

Mark 3:5-6

Mark 3:22

Mark 5:17

5. Fight and/or War

Mark 10:32-34

"Settle matters quickly with your adversary who is taking you to court. Do it while you are still together on the way, or your adversary may hand you over to the judge, and the judge may hand you over to the officer, and you may be thrown into prison.
Matthew 5:25 (NIV)

Types of Conflict
Negative vs. Positive Approaches to Conflict

Avoidance vs. Active Engagement

Avoidance: Physical, mental, emotional engagement

Active: Physical, mental, emotional disengagement

Force vs. Talk

Force: Can be physical or verbal. The result is the real issue is never resolved and new issues are created because of the force.

Talk: Openness, stressing areas of agreement. The result is the intentional discovery of common ground.

Blame vs. Empathy

Blame: Avoiding the real issue at hand by becoming personal. For example, someone may voice a phrase like, "This is the type of thing I'd expect from a person like you." The result is the conflict becomes about the person and not the content.

Empathy: Expressing genuine interest in the viewpoint of the other party. The result is the creation of increased, common understanding.

Gunnysacking vs. Present Focus

Gunnysacking: The saving up of grievances with the intention of unloading them during the conflict.

Present Focus: Looking at the issue at hand in an immediate, timely fashion. The result is that the conflict stays centered on content and not the relationship.

Personal Rejection vs. Acceptance

Personal Rejection: Withholding love and affection through actions or words which are cold and uncaring. Attacks the self worth of the other person.

Acceptance: The expression of positive feeling toward the other party as a person.

Types of Conflict

Steps to resolving conflict

1. Define the conflict.

- Stay content focused and identify the root of the issue.

- Avoid abstract statements and work to define the point of difference.

- Examine the issue from the other person's perspective.

- Do not attempt to read their mind. Instead, ask them to share.

- Confirm their perspective. Do not assume you understand them.

- Note: "Confirming" is different than affirming or agreeing with them. It simply means you understand where they are coming from.

2. Examine possible solutions.

- Look for solutions that are win-win.

- Solutions based on winning and losing cause frustration and resentment.

- Weigh the costs and the benefits of the proposed solution.

- Keep in mind the mission and shared purpose of the team.

3. Try the solution.

- Ask if the solution is working for both sides.

- Ask how both sides will feel about the solution in a few days.

4. Examine the result.

- Discuss with each other whether or not the situation seems better?

- Ask each other, "Are we better positioned to accomplish our common mission?"

- Talk together during a time when emotions are not at the forefront.

5. Accept or reject the solution.

- If the solution is not succeeding, then return to step one and work toward a different solution.

Application:

- What step do you think is most commonly skipped in this process?

- What effect or impact does missing that step have on the team achieving a resolution?

Types of Conflict

Keys to resolving conflict

Before Conflict

1. Seek privacy.

   Why?

   - Because when others are present, more problems are created.

   - Totally honesty cannot be reached.

   - Attempts are made to protect personal images.

   - Embarrassment occurs.

2. Know the issue and define the specific problem or disagreement.

   Why?

   - Because assuming only gets us in trouble and confusion leads to relational conflict.

   - We must always remember to clarify the content of our disagreement.

3. Agree to find a solution.

   Why?

   - Because some people simply enjoy conflict for the sake of conflict while others simply want to watch you lose.

   - If you are not working toward a solution, then you are creating more problems.

   - Often in anger, people try to vent their feelings, not solve the conflict.

After Conflict

4. Learn from the conflict.

   Why?

   - Because history repeats itself and if you did not learn then you are destined to repeat the same mistakes.

5. Assess strategies.

   - Learn what worked.

   - Learn what did not work.

   - If you did not learn, then the conflict was wasted.

6. Keep perspective on the conflict.

   - Do not view your relationship through the eyes of conflict.

7. Attack negative feelings and affirm the resolution.

   - Make up!

   - Remember in positive healthy conflict the goal is not to beat the other person but to utilze the conflict to make each other better.

   - Feelings of personal rejection or the use of negative tactics can linger if we do not acknowledge them and address them assertively.

Types of Conflict
Negative vs. Positive Approaches to Conflict

Reflection

The key concept in understanding the different approaches to conflict is that the negative methods are typically associated with abusive tactics that result in relational conflict. In contrast, the positive approaches focus on the content or the issue at hand.

Respond

What have been your experiences with different forms of conflict?

What did you find most insightful or helpful?

What techniques do you find yourself using most often?

What areas do you commit to work on or actions steps do you plan to take?

Summative assessment:

How does the world challenge my faith?

Memory verse:

"But in your hearts revere Christ as Lord. Always be prepared to give an answer to everyone who asks you to give the reason for the hope that you have. But do this with gentleness and respect."

- 1 Peter 3:15, NIV

Part 1. Discussion Board

How do you feel the world challenges your faith? Give three examples.

Part one: Reply to the discussion board.

Part two: Reply to two of your peers.

Part three: Synthesize your thoughts and incorporate them into the introduction of your unit reflection paper.

Part II. Reflection paper

According to 1 Peter 3:15, we should "always be prepared to give an answer to everyone who asks [us] to give the reason for the hope that [we] have. But do this with gentleness and respect." Using the Bible Department guidelines for a one-page paper, write a one-page paper answering the following questions.

1. How do you feel the world challenges your faith? Give three examples. In light of this, how prepared are you to obey this command at this point in your life?

2. What area do you need to work on this semester? (e.g., becoming more "prepared," becoming more secure in "the hope that you have," answering with "gentleness and respect")

   Explain. Formulate a S.M.A.R.T. goal for yourself as a commitment to what you want to get out of this course. A S.M.A.R.T. Goal is something that is:

      Specific – Be as specific as possible.
      Measureable – How will you know when you've accomplished it?
      Attainable – Is it realistic? Are you challenging yourself?
      Relational – What relationships will be impacted by this? How?
      Time-Bound – When would you accomplish this by?

3. How would obeying this verse help to dispel the faulty concept in some non-believers' minds that faith is "believing something you know isn't true"?

Format: Use the one-page Bible paper template and format.

Examine™
SPIRITUAL FORMATION TOOL
ChristCenteredDiscipleship.com

*"Everyone ought to examine themselves
before they eat of the bread and drink from
the cup."*
1 Corinthians 11:28, NLT

Wheaton Press
Read. Respond. Reflect.™

Where are you?
Read. Respond. Reflect.

Directions: *Read through the verses below and highlight or underline any words or phrases that seem to reflect or resonate with where you are at.*

Skeptic. Presented with the person of Christ and the gospel multiple times, I demonstrate disinterest or unbelief.

> "Even after Jesus had performed so many signs in their presence, they still would not believe in him." John 12:37, NIV

Characteristics: Calloused heart, dull ears, closed eyes.

> "[F]or this people's heart has grown callous, their ears are dull of hearing, they have closed their eyes." Matthew 13:15a, WEB

Christ's Next-Step Invitation: Repent. Believe.

> "Then he began to denounce the cities in which most of his mighty works had been done, because they didn't repent." Matthew 11:20 ,WEB

Growth Barrier: A lack of spiritual understanding.

> "When anyone hears the message about the kingdom and does not understand it, the evil one comes and snatches away what was sown in their heart. This is the seed sown along the path." Matthew 13:19, NIV

Spiritual Need: A loving and praying friend, a change of mind and heart initiated by the Holy Spirit.

> "He said to them, 'This kind can come out by nothing, except by prayer and fasting.'" Mark 9:29, WEB

> "As for you, you were dead in your transgressions and sins, in which you used to live when you followed the ways of this world and of the ruler of the kingdom of the air, the spirit who is now at work in those who are disobedient." Ephesians 2:1-2, NIV

Seeker. Questioning, with a desire to learn more about Jesus.

> "He answered, 'And who is he, sir? Tell me, so that I may believe in him.'" John 9:36, ISV

Characteristics: A ready heart, open ears, questions with an interest to learn more about Jesus.

> "Again, the next day, John was standing with two of his disciples, and he looked at Jesus as he walked, and said, 'Behold, the Lamb of God!' The two disciples heard him speak, and they followed Jesus. Jesus turned, and saw them following, and said to them, 'What are you looking for?' They said to him, 'Rabbi' (which is to say, being interpreted, Teacher), 'where are you staying?' He said to them, 'Come, and see.' They came and saw where he was staying, and they stayed with him that day. It was about the tenth hour." John 1:35-39, WEB

Christ's Next-Step Invitation: Repent. Believe.

> "Now after John was taken into custody, Jesus came into Galilee, preaching the Good News of God's Kingdom, and saying, 'The time is fulfilled, and God's Kingdom is at hand! Repent, and believe in the Good News.'" Mark 1:14-15, WEB

Growth Barrier: A lack of clear presentation and understanding of the Gospel, a lack of invitation.

> "How, then, can people call on someone they have not believed? And how can they believe in someone they have not heard about? And how can they hear without someone preaching?" Romans 10:14, ISV

Spiritual Need: A clear gospel presentation and an invitation to believe and receive salvation.

> "But to all who did receive him, who believed in his name, he gave the right to become children of God." John 1:12, ESV

Believer. Presented with the Gospel I believe.

> He said, "Lord, I believe!" and he worshiped him. John 9:38 (WEB).

Characteristics: Seed begins to germinate, shallow soil, little or no roots.

> Other seeds fell on rocky ground, where they did not have much soil, and immediately they sprang up, since they had no depth of soil, but when the sun rose they were scorched. And since they had no root, they withered away. Matthew 13:5-6

Christ's Next Step Invitation: Follow.

> And he said to them, "Follow me, and I will make you fishers of men." Matthew 4:19 (ESV).

Growth Barrier: Lack of roots, lack of knowledge, testing, trouble, persecution.

> These in the same way are those who are sown on the rocky places, who, when they have heard the word, immediately receive it with joy. They have no root in themselves, but are short-lived. When oppression or persecution arises because of the word, immediately they stumble. Mark 4:16-17 (WEB).

Spiritual Need: Prayer, roots, knowledge, biblical teaching, time, worship and someone to walk with them.

> Like newborn infants, long for the pure spiritual milk, that by it you may grow up into salvation. 1 Peter 2:2 (ESV).

> So then, just as you received Christ Jesus as Lord, continue to live your lives in him, rooted and built up in him, strengthened in the faith as you were taught, and overflowing with thankfulness. Colossians 2:6-7 (NIV).

> We continually ask God to fill you with the knowledge of His will through all the wisdom and understanding that the Spirit gives, so that you may live a life worthy of the Lord and please Him in every way: bearing fruit in every good work, growing in the knowledge of God, being strengthened with all power according to His glorious might so that you may have great endurance and patience, and giving joyful thanks to the Father, who has qualified you to share in the inheritance of His holy people in the kingdom of light. Colossians 1:9-12 (NIV).

Follower. Growing in faith and love; deepening roots and knowledge; struggling with thorns, trials, forgiveness, doubt, and perseverance.

"By this all people will know that you are my disciples, if you have love for one another." John 13:35, ESV

Characteristics: Beginning to push through the soil, struggling with thorns and weeds.

"Others fell among thorns. The thorns grew up and choked them." Matthew 13:7, WEB

"And calling the crowd to him with his disciples, he said to them, 'If anyone would come after me, let him deny himself and take up his cross and follow me.'" Mark 8:34, ESV

Christ's Next-Step Invitation: Deny self; pick up cross; trust, obey, and love Christ and others.

"Then Jesus said to his disciples, "If anyone desires to come after me, let him deny himself, and take up his cross, and follow me." Matthew 16:24, WEB

Growth Barrier: Thorns, worries of this life, doubt, deceitfulness of wealth, comfort, self and self-will.

"Others are those who are sown among the thorns. These are those who have heard the word, and the cares of this age, and the deceitfulness of riches, and the lusts of other things entering in choke the word, and it becomes unfruitful." Mark 4:18-19,

Spiritual Need: Deny self; trials; endurance, perseverance, time, small group relationships, and accountability.

"Consider it pure joy, my brothers and sisters, whenever you face trials of many kinds, because you know that the testing of your faith produces perseverance. Let perseverance finish its work so that you may be mature and complete, not lacking anything." James 1:2-4, NIV

"Through him we have also obtained access by faith into this grace in which we stand, and we rejoice in hope of the glory of God. Not only that, but we rejoice in our sufferings, knowing that suffering produces endurance, and endurance produces character, and character produces hope." Romans 5:2-4, ESV

"These have come so that the proven genuineness of your faith—of greater worth than gold, which perishes even though refined by fire—may result in praise, glory and honor when Jesus Christ is revealed." 1 Peter 1:7, NIV

Friend. Marked by obedient love for Christ and others; may wrestle with isolation, complacency and accountability.

"You are my friends if you do what I command you." John 15:14, ESV

Characteristics: Good soil, obedience to Christ, fruit, growing faith, increasing love and perseverance in trials.

"We ought always to thank God for you, brothers and sisters, and rightly so, because your faith is growing more and more, and the love all of you have for one another is increasing. Therefore, among God's churches we boast about your perseverance and faith in all the persecutions and trials you are enduring." 2 Thessalonians 1:3-4, NIV

Christ's Next-Step Invitation: Love, obey, go, teach.

"If you love me, you will keep my commandments." John 14:15, ESV

"Jesus came to them and spoke to them, saying, 'All authority has been given to me in heaven and on earth. Go, and make disciples of all nations, baptizing them in the name of the Father and of the Son and of the Holy Spirit, teaching them to observe all things that I commanded you. Behold, I am with you always, even to the end of the age.' Amen." Matthew 28:18-20,

Growth Barrier: Complacency, fear, pride, lack of vision and lack of equipping.

"Then he said to his disciples, 'The harvest indeed is plentiful, but the laborers are few.'" Matthew 9:37, WEB

"How, then, can people call on someone they have not believed? And how can they believe in someone they have not heard about? And how can they hear without someone preaching?" Romans 10:14, ISV

Spiritual Need: Vision, continued obedience, equipping, empowerment, continued spurring and accountability within community.

" … to equip his people for works of service, so that the body of Christ may be built up until we all reach unity in the faith and in the knowledge of the Son of God and become mature, attaining to the whole measure of the fullness of Christ." Ephesians 4:12-13, NIV

"As for you, brothers, do not grow weary in doing good." 2 Thessalonians 3:13, ESV

"Let us continue to hold firmly to the hope that we confess without wavering, for the one who made the promise is faithful. And let us continue to consider how to motivate one another to love and good deeds, not neglecting to meet together, as is the habit of some, but encouraging one another even more as you see the day of the Lord coming nearer." Hebrews 10:23-25, ISV

Fisherman. Reflecting Christ and reproducing fruit of righteousness and good works.

"Because we have heard of your faith in Christ Jesus and of the love you have for all God's people—the faith and love that spring from the hope stored up for you in heaven and about which you have already heard in the true message of the gospel that has come to you. In the same way, the gospel is bearing fruit and growing throughout the whole world—just as it has been doing among you since the day you heard it and truly understood God's grace." Colossians 1:4-6, NIV

Characteristics: Good soil, fruitfulness, harvest, influence, reflecting Christ.

"Others fell on good soil, and yielded fruit: some one hundred times as much, some sixty, and some thirty." Matthew 13:8, WEB

Christ's Next-Step Invitation: Teach others.

"Therefore, as you go, disciple people in all nations, baptizing them in the name of the Father, and the Son, and the Holy Spirit, teaching them to obey everything that I've commanded you." Matthew 28:19-20a, ISV

Growth Barrier: Complacency, fear, pride, lack of vision, lack of equipping, weariness.

"Let's not get tired of doing what is good, for at the right time we will reap a harvest—if we do not give up." Galatians 6:9, ISV

"Think about the one who endured such hostility from sinners, so that you may not become tired and give up." Hebrews 12:3,

Spiritual Need: Perseverance, humility, faithfulness, accountability, reliable people.

"It gave me great joy when some believers came and testified about your faithfulness to the truth, telling how you continue to walk in it." 3 John 3, NIV

"And what you have heard from me in the presence of many witnesses entrust to faithful men who will be able to teach others also." 2 Timothy 2:2, ESV

Examine™ Spiritual Formation Planning Tool

More resources available at WheatonPress.com

Directions: Answer the following seven questions using the words or phrases you highlighted or underlined.

1. Where am I?

Skeptic. When presented with the gospel, I do not believe.

Seeker. Questioning, with a desire to learn more about Jesus.

Believer. Presented with the gospel, I chose to believe.

Follower. Growing in faith, love, and roots. Struggling with thorns, trials, and perseverance.

Friend. Marked by obedient love for Christ and others.

Fisherman. Reflecting Christ and bearing fruit of righteousness and good works.

2. Where would I like to be in six months?

Skeptic. When presented with the gospel, I do not believe.

Seeker. Questioning, with a desire to learn more about Jesus.

Believer. Presented with the Gospel, I chose to believe.

Follower. Growing in faith, love, and roots. Struggling with thorns, trials, and perseverance.

Friend. Marked by obedient love for Christ and others.

Fisherman. Reflecting Christ and bearing fruit of righteousness and good works.

3. What invitation do I need to respond to in order to take my next step?

Skeptic. Repent.

Seeker. Repent. Believe.

Believer. Follow.

Follower. Deny self. Pick up cross. Obey. Love Christ and others.

Friend. Love. Obey. Go.

Fisherman. Teach others.

4. What barriers will I face?

Skeptic. Calloused heart, deaf ears, closed eyes.

Seeker. Lack of clear testimony. Lack of invitation.

Believer. Lack of root. Testing. Trouble. Persecution.

Follower. Thorns. Worries of this life. Deceitfulness of wealth. Comfort. Self.

Friend. Complacency. Fear. Lack of vision. Lack of equipping.

Fisherman. Complacency. Fear. Lack of vision. Lack of equipping. Weariness.

5. What spiritual needs do I have?

Skeptic. Prayer. Repentance. A believing friend.

Seeker. Receive. Believe. Salvation.

Believer. Prayer. Roots. Knowledge. Teaching. Worship. Time.

Follower. Deny self. Trials. Endurance. Perseverance. Time. Small group relationships and accountability.

Friend. Vision. Continued obedience. Equipping. Opportunity. Empowerment. Accountability within community.

Fisherman. Perseverance. Faithfulness. Reliable people.

6. What steps will I take?

7. Who will I ask to hold me accountable?

Revelation

Doctrine & Apologetics

Unit Essential Questions

1. Has God revealed Himself?

2. What is general revelation?

3. What difference does it make in my life?

Reading

Know Why You Believe, Chapters 5, 9
Know What You Believe, Chapter 1

Unit Learning Assessments

Summative:

Socratic Dialogue
Position paper

Daily Learning Plan

2.1　Does science silence God or do science and scripture agree?

2.2　What is General revelation?

2.3　Does God really hold people accountable for General revelation?
　　　If God, then why evil?

2.4　Can either evolution or Genesis be trusted?

2.5　How do I write a Theological position paper?

2.6　How do I write a personal doctrinal statement?
　　　How do I write a personal apologetic?

2.7　How do I communicate my theological beliefs?

Does science silence God or do silence and scripture agree?

Am I prepared to meet the challenge beyond the walls?

Revelation
Reading notes

Know What You Believe, Chapter 1: The Bible

Definitions:

- Plenary: all of Scripture is inspired, not merely some parts.

- Verbal: indicates that inspiration extends to the words of the Bible themselves, not only to the ideas.

- Literal

Know Why You Believe, Chapter 5: Is the Bible God's Word?

Definitions:

- Inspiration: God so superintended the writers of Scripture that they wrote what he wanted them to write, disclosing the exact truth he wanted to convey.
- Inerrancy
    unfailable

Essential questions:

1. According to the scriptural use of the word "inspired," how is the Bible's inspiration different from the inspiration of Shakespeare's plays?

    The Bible's inspiration is different from inspiration of Shakespeare's plays by the words of the Bible being "outbreathed" (from the mouth of God). The words did not come from the writers themselves.

2. The author suggests that a clear definition of inerrancy is needed (p. 65). How would you define the term?   Unfailable

3. Are there any ways you need to redirect your thinking in order to take the Bible the way God intends it?

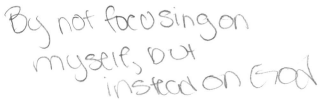

By not focusing on myself, but instead on God

Revelation
Reading notes

Know Why You Believe, Chapter 6: Are the Bible documents reliable?

- What questions about reliability of the Bible could you relate to the most?

  The questions about reliability of the Bible that I could relate to the most were what difference does the historical accuracy of the Bible make? and what guarantee do we have that deletions and embellishments have not totally obscured the original

- Which answers offered in this unit helped to resolve those questions for you? message of the Bible.

  The answers offered in this unit that helped to resolve my questions were

- What questions still remain unanswered in your mind?

  Some questions that still remain unanswered in my mind are How do we know that the Biblical documents we have today are a part of the original manuscripts?

- If you have unanswered questions, what is your specific strategy for pursuing the answers?

  My specific strategy for pursing the answers include inductive research on the Bible and its

Can evolution or Genesis be trusted?

Can evolution or Genesis be trusted?

Revelation
Class notes

Summative assessment
Position paper outline

What I believe:

Why do I believe it?

What difference will it make in my life?

Bibliology

Doctrine & Apologetics
INVITED TO GO AND TEACH

Unit Essential Questions

1. Is the Bible God's Word?

2. Are the biblical documents reliable?

3. What difference will that make in my life?

Reading

Know What You Believe, Chapter 1

Know Why You Believe, Chapters 6, 7, 9

Unit Learning Assessments

Summative:

Position paper

Daily Learning Plan

3.1　Is the Bible God's Word?

3.2　Are the Biblical documents reliable?

3.3　Can God's Word be trusted?
　　　Did God really say…?

3.4　What is textual criticism?
　　　What passages are not in the Bible?

3.5　What do I believe, can I trust the Bible?

3.6　Why do I believe is it reasonable to trust the Bible?

Bibliology
YouTube Friday

63

Bibliology
Reading notes

Know What You Believe, Chapter 1
The Bible

Definitions:

- Plenary

- Verbal

- Literal

Know Why You Believe, Chapter 6:
Are the Bible documents reliable?

Know Why You Believe, Chapter 7:
Does Archaeology Verify Scripture?

> Of the archaeological findings mentioned
> in this chapter, which did you find to be
> most interesting and impressive? Explain
> your answer.

Did God really say?

Can I trust the Bible?

Summative assessment
Position paper notes

What I believe:

Why do I believe it?

What difference will it make in my life?

Theology proper

Doctrine & Apologetics

INVITED TO GO AND TEACH

Unit Essential Questions

1. Is there a God?

2. How (and why) has He chosen to reveal Himself to us?

3. What difference will that make in my life?

Reading

Know What You Believe, Chapter 2

Know Why You Believe, Chapter 2

Unit Learning Assessments

Summative:

Position paper

Daily Learning Plan

4.1   Does God exist? What are the arguments for the existence of God?

4.2   What are the revealed attributes of God?

4.3   What are the practical implications of the description of the Trinity found in Ephesians 1?

4.4   Mini-Project Presentations

Theology Proper
YouTube Friday

Theology Proper

Reading notes

Know What You Believe, Chapter 2: God

Definitions:

- Trinity

1. Explain this statement: "God is one being, but He exists in three persons."

2. How do the members of the Trinity relate to each other?

3. What is the difference between God's directive will and His permissive will? What biblical passages support your explanation?

Theology Proper
Does God exist?

Know Why You Believe, Chapter 2: Is there a God?

Definitions:

- Anthropology

1. Explain the argument for God's existence based on the law of cause and effect (p. 24-25).

2. Explain the theory of "infinite time plus chance" (pp. 25-27).

3. Explain the "moral argument" for the existence of God (pp. 32-33).

Know Why You Believe, Chapter 2: Is there a God?

4. How would you argue for or against the moral argument?

5. Which of the arguments for God's existence seem most helpful to you in explaining the plausibility of God's existence? Why?

6. Which one seems least helpful? Why?

Summative assessment
Position paper notes

What I believe:

Why do I believe it?

What difference will it make in my life?

Christology

Doctrine & Apologetics
INVITED TO GO AND TEACH

Unit Essential Questions

1. Is Christ God?

2. Did Jesus claim to be God?

3. What are the practical implications of the Incarnation and hypostatic union?

4. Did Jesus rise from the dead?

Reading

Know Why You Believe, Chapters 3-4

Know What You Believe, Chapters 3-4

Unit Learning Assessments

Summative:

Position paper

Daily Learning Plan

5.1   Can the resurrection be trusted?

5.2   Did Jesus claim to be God?

5.3   Luke 2:52 project. What was Jesus like as a child?

5.4   What difference does Jesus make?

Christology
YouTube Friday

75

Christology

Reading notes

Know What You Believe, Chapter 3: Jesus Christ

Definitions:

- Incarnation

- Hypostatic union

- Kenosis

- Theophany

- Christophany

1. List and explain four ways in which Jesus proved He is fully God.

    •

    •

    •

    •

2. How do we know Jesus was also fully human?

3. Why does it matter that Jesus was fully human?

4. What are three reasons Jesus had to live a perfect life?

    •

    •

    •

5. Now that Jesus has ascended to heaven, what roles does He assume?

Christology

Reading Notes

Know What You Believe, Chapter 4: Jesus Christ's Death

Definitions:

- Atonement

- Appeasement

- Ransom

- Substitution

- Reconciliation

1. How did Christ's death fulfill the Old Testament sacrificial system?

2. How would you answer a friend who asked you, "How could one person die to save the whole world?"

Know Why You Believe, Chapter 3: Is Christ God?

Many people claim Jesus was a "great moral teacher" but not the Son of God. How would you answer such a person?

Know Why You Believe, Chapter 4: Did Christ rise from the dead?

1. Read Matthew 28:11-15. Even Jesus' enemies admitted His tomb was empty. The truth of Christ's resurrection rests on how the tomb was emptied. The authorities clamed that Jesus' followers removed the body. Other explanations often given: that the authorities moved the body, or the disciples returned to the wrong tomb (p. 51). What makes these explanations reasonable or unreasonable?

2. How has your life been changed by belief in the Resurrection?

Summative assessment
Position paper notes

What I believe:

Why do I believe it?

What difference will it make in my life?

Pneumatology

Doctrine & Apologetics
INVITED TO GO AND TEACH

Unit Essential Questions

1. Why is it important to know the Holy Spirit is a personality?

2. What is the practical role of the Holy Spirit in the Trinity?

3. When are we sealed, indwelt, and baptized by the Holy Spirit?

4. How did Christ relate to the Holy Spirit? How can we apply and imitate His example?

Reading

Know What You Believe, Chapter 4

1 Corinthians

Unit Learning Assessments

Summative:

Position paper

Daily Learning Plan

6.1 Why is it important to understand that the Holy Spirit is a personality?
What is the practical role of the Holy Spirit in the Trinity?

6.2 When are we sealed, indwelt, and baptized by the Holy Spirit?
How did the Holy Spirit interact with believers in the Old and New Testaments?

6.3 How did Christ relate to the Holy Spirit, and how does His example apply
to my life?

6.4 What are the practical implications of the description of the Trinity found
in Ephesians 1?

Pneumatology
Reading notes

Know What You Believe, Chapter 6: The Holy Spirit

Why is it important to know the Holy Spirit is a personality?

List and explain five aspects of the Holy Spirit's work in the Old Testament.

Explain this statement: "In the Old Testament, the Holy Spirit came on individuals temporarily."

Describe the New Testament arrival of the Holy Spirit. How does this compare to the arrival of the Holy Spirit in the Old Testament? What was God's purpose for the similarity or difference?

When are we sealed, indwelt, and baptized by the Holy Spirit?

Pneumatology
Intro to 1 Corinthians

1 Corinthians

1 Corinthians 1

Appeal to Unity

1 Paul, called as an apostle of Jesus Christ by the will of God, and Sosthenes our brother,
2 To the church of God which is at Corinth, to those who have been sanctified in Christ Jesus, saints by calling, with all who in every place call on the name of our Lord Jesus Christ, their Lord and ours:
3 Grace to you and peace from God our Father and the Lord Jesus Christ.
4 I thank my God always concerning you for the grace of God which was given you in Christ Jesus, 5 that in everything you were enriched in Him, in all speech and all knowledge, 6 even as the testimony concerning Christ was confirmed in you, 7 so that you are not lacking in any gift, awaiting eagerly the revelation of our Lord Jesus Christ, 8 who will also confirm you to the end, blameless in the day of our Lord Jesus Christ.
9 God is faithful, through whom you were called into fellowship with His Son, Jesus Christ our Lord.
10 Now I exhort you, brethren, by the name of our Lord Jesus Christ, that you all agree and that there be no divisions among you, but that you be made complete in the same mind and in the same judgment. 11 For I have been informed concerning you, my brethren, by Chloe's people, that there are quarrels among you. 12 Now I mean this, that each one of you is saying, "I am of Paul," and "I of Apollos," and "I of Cephas," and "I of Christ." 13 Has Christ been divided? Paul was not crucified for you, was he? Or were you baptized in the name of Paul? 14 I thank God that I baptized none of you except Crispus and Gaius, 15 so that no one would say you were baptized in my name. 16 Now I did baptize also the household of Stephanas; beyond that, I do not know whether I baptized any other. 17 For Christ did not send me to baptize, but to preach the gospel, not in cleverness of speech, so that the cross of Christ would not be made void.

The Wisdom of God

18 For the word of the cross is foolishness to those who are perishing, but to us who are being saved it is the power of God. 19 For it is written,
"I will destroy the wisdom of the wise,
And the cleverness of the clever I will set aside."
20 Where is the wise man? Where is the scribe? Where is the debater of this age? Has not God made foolish the wisdom of the world? 21 For since in the wisdom of God the world through its wisdom did not come to know God, God was well-pleased through the foolishness of the message preached to save those who believe.
22 For indeed Jews ask for signs and Greeks search for wisdom; 23 but we preach Christ crucified, to Jews a stumbling block and to Gentiles foolishness, 24 but to those who are the called, both Jews and Greeks, Christ the power of God and the wisdom of God. 25 Because the foolishness of God is wiser than men, and the weakness of God is stronger than men.
26 For consider your calling, brethren, that there were not many wise according to the flesh, not many mighty, not many noble; 27 but God has chosen the foolish things of the world to shame the wise, and God has chosen the weak things of the world to shame the things which are strong, 28 and the base things of the world and the despised God has chosen, the things that are not, so that He may nullify the things that are, 29 so that no man may boast before God. 30 But by His doing you are in Christ Jesus, who became to us wisdom from God, and righteousness and sanctification, and redemption, 31 so that, just as it is written, "Let him who boasts, boast in the Lord."

83

1 Corinthians

1 Corinthians 2

Paul's Reliance upon the Spirit

2 And when I came to you, brethren, I did not come with superiority of speech or of wisdom, proclaiming to you the testimony of God. 2 For I determined to know nothing among you except Jesus Christ, and Him crucified. 3 I was with you in weakness and in fear and in much trembling, 4 and my message and my preaching were not in persuasive words of wisdom, but in demonstration of the Spirit and of power, 5 so that your faith would not rest on the wisdom of men, but on the power of God.

6 Yet we do speak wisdom among those who are mature; a wisdom, however, not of this age nor of the rulers of this age, who are passing away; 7 but we speak God's wisdom in a mystery, the hidden wisdom which God predestined before the ages to our glory; 8 the wisdom which none of the rulers of this age has understood; for if they had understood it they would not have crucified the Lord of glory!

9 but just as it is written,

"Things which eye has not seen and ear has not heard,

And which have not entered the heart of man,

All that God has prepared for those who love Him."

10 For to us God revealed them through the Spirit; for the Spirit searches all things, even the depths of God.

11 For who among men knows the thoughts of a man except the spirit of the man which is in him? Even so the thoughts of God no one knows except the Spirit of God. 12 Now we have received, not the spirit of the world, but the Spirit who is from God, so that we may know the things freely given to us by God, 13 which things we also speak, not in words taught by human wisdom, but in those taught by the Spirit, combining spiritual thoughts with spiritual words. 14 But a natural man does not accept the things of the Spirit of God, for they are foolishness to him; and he cannot understand them, because they are spiritually appraised. 15 But he who is spiritual appraises all things, yet he himself is appraised by no one. 16 For who has known the mind of the Lord, that he will instruct Him? But we have the mind of Christ.

1 Corinthians

1 Corinthians 3

3 And I, brethren, could not speak to you as to spiritual men, but as to men of flesh, as to infants in Christ. 2 I gave you milk to drink, not solid food; for you were not yet able to receive it. Indeed, even now you are not yet able, 3 for you are still fleshly. For since there is jealousy and strife among you, are you not fleshly, and are you not walking like mere men? 4 For when one says, "I am of Paul," and another, "I am of Apollos," are you not mere men?

5 What then is Apollos? And what is Paul? Servants through whom you believed, even as the Lord gave opportunity to each one. 6 I planted, Apollos watered, but God was causing the growth. 7 So then neither the one who plants nor the one who waters is anything, but God who causes the growth. 8 Now he who plants and he who waters are one; but each will receive his own reward according to his own labor. 9 For we are God's fellow workers; you are God's field, God's building.

10 According to the grace of God which was given to me, like a wise master builder I laid a foundation, and another is building on it. But each man must be careful how he builds on it. 11 For no man can lay a foundation other than the one which is laid, which is Jesus Christ.

12 Now if any man builds on the foundation with gold, silver, precious stones, wood, hay, straw, 13 each man's work will become evident; for the day will show it because it is to be revealed with fire, and the fire itself will test the quality of each man's work. 14 If any man's work which he has built on it remains, he will receive a reward. 15 If any man's work is burned up, he will suffer loss; but he himself will be saved, yet so as through fire.

16 Do you not know that you are a temple of God and that the Spirit of God dwells in you? 17 If any man destroys the temple of God, God will destroy him, for the temple of God is holy, and that is what you are.

18 Let no man deceive himself. If any man among you thinks that he is wise in this age, he must become foolish, so that he may become wise. 19 For the wisdom of this world is foolishness before God. For it is written, "He is the one who catches the wise in their craftiness"; 20 and again, "The Lord knows the reasonings of the wise, that they are useless." 21 So then let no one boast in men. For all things belong to you, 22 whether Paul or Apollos or Cephas or the world or life or death or things present or things to come; all things belong to you, 23 and you belong to Christ; and Christ belongs to God.

85

1 Corinthians

1 Corinthians 4

4 Let a man regard us in this manner, as servants of Christ and stewards of the mysteries of God. 2 In this case, moreover, it is required of stewards that one be found trustworthy. 3 But to me it is a very small thing that I may be examined by you, or by any human court; in fact, I do not even examine myself. 4 For I am conscious of nothing against myself, yet I am not by this acquitted; but the one who examines me is the Lord.

5 Therefore do not go on passing judgment before the time, but wait until the Lord comes who will both bring to light the things hidden in the darkness and disclose the motives of men's hearts; and then each man's praise will come to him from God.

6 Now these things, brethren, I have figuratively applied to myself and Apollos for your sakes, so that in us you may learn not to exceed what is written, so that no one of you will become arrogant in behalf of one against the other. 7 For who regards you as superior? What do you have that you did not receive? And if you did receive it, why do you boast as if you had not received it?

8 You are already filled, you have already become rich, you have become kings without us; and indeed, I wish that you had become kings so that we also might reign with you.

9 For, I think, God has exhibited us apostles last of all, as men condemned to death; because we have become a spectacle to the world, both to angels and to men.

10 We are fools for Christ's sake, but you are prudent in Christ; we are weak, but you are strong; you are distinguished, but we are without honor. 11 To this present hour we are both hungry and thirsty, and are poorly clothed, and are roughly treated, and are homeless; 12 and we toil, working with our own hands; when we are reviled, we bless; when we are persecuted, we endure; 13 when we are slandered, we try to conciliate; we have become as the scum of the world, the dregs of all things, even until now.

14 I do not write these things to shame you, but to admonish you as my beloved children. 15 For if you were to have countless tutors in Christ, yet you would not have many fathers, for in Christ Jesus I became your father through the gospel. 16 Therefore I exhort you, be imitators of me. 17 For this reason I have sent to you Timothy, who is my beloved and faithful child in the Lord, and he will remind you of my ways which are in Christ, just as I teach everywhere in every church. 18 Now some have become arrogant, as though I were not coming to you. 19 But I will come to you soon, if the Lord wills, and I shall find out, not the words of those who are arrogant but their power. 20 For the kingdom of God does not consist in words but in power. 21 What do you desire? Shall I come to you with a rod, or with love and a spirit of gentleness?

1 Corinthians

1 Corinthians 5

Immorality Rebuked

5 It is actually reported that there is immorality among you, and immorality of such a kind as does not exist even among the Gentiles, that someone has his father's wife. 2 You have become arrogant and have not mourned instead, so that the one who had done this deed would be removed from your midst.
3 For I, on my part, though absent in body but present in spirit, have already judged him who has so committed this, as though I were present. 4 In the name of our Lord Jesus, when you are assembled, and I with you in spirit, with the power of our Lord Jesus, 5 I have decided to deliver such a one to Satan for the destruction of his flesh, so that his spirit may be saved in the day of the Lord Jesus.
6 Your boasting is not good. Do you not know that a little leaven leavens the whole lump of dough?

7 Clean out the old leaven so that you may be a new lump, just as you are in fact unleavened. For Christ our Passover also has been sacrificed.
8 Therefore let us celebrate the feast, not with old leaven, nor with the leaven of malice and wickedness, but with the unleavened bread of sincerity and truth.
9 I wrote you in my letter not to associate with immoral people; 10 I did not at all mean with the immoral people of this world, or with the covetous and swindlers, or with idolaters, for then you would have to go out of the world. 11 But actually, I wrote to you not to associate with any so-called brother if he is an immoral person, or covetous, or an idolater, or a reviler, or a drunkard, or a swindler—not even to eat with such a one. 12 For what have I to do with judging outsiders? Do you not judge those who are within the church? 13 But those who are outside, God judges. Remove the wicked man from among yourselves.

1 Corinthians

1 Corinthians 6

Lawsuits Discouraged

6 Does any one of you, when he has a case against his neighbor, dare to go to law before the unrighteous and not before the saints? 2 Or do you not know that the saints will judge the world? If the world is judged by you, are you not competent to constitute the smallest law courts? 3 Do you not know that we will judge angels? How much more matters of this life? 4 So if you have law courts dealing with matters of this life, do you appoint them as judges who are of no account in the church? 5 I say this to your shame. Is it so, that there is not among you one wise man who will be able to decide between his brethren, 6 but brother goes to law with brother, and that before unbelievers?

7 Actually, then, it is already a defeat for you, that you have lawsuits with one another. Why not rather be wronged? Why not rather be defrauded? 8 On the contrary, you yourselves wrong and defraud. You do this even to your brethren.

9 Or do you not know that the unrighteous will not inherit the kingdom of God? Do not be deceived; neither fornicators, nor idolaters, nor adulterers, nor effeminate, nor homosexuals, 10 nor thieves, nor the covetous, nor drunkards, nor revilers, nor swindlers, will inherit the kingdom of God. 11 Such were some of you; but you were washed, but you were sanctified, but you were justified in the name of the Lord Jesus Christ and in the Spirit of our God.

The Body Is the Lord's

12 All things are lawful for me, but not all things are profitable. All things are lawful for me, but I will not be mastered by anything. 13 Food is for the stomach and the stomach is for food, but God will do away with both of them. Yet the body is not for immorality, but for the Lord, and the Lord is for the body. 14 Now God has not only raised the Lord, but will also raise us up through His power. 15 Do you not know that your bodies are members of Christ? Shall I then take away the members of Christ and make them members of a prostitute? May it never be! 16 Or do you not know that the one who joins himself to a prostitute is one body with her? For He says, "The two shall become one flesh." 17 But the one who joins himself to the Lord is one spirit with Him. 18 Flee immorality. Every other sin that a man commits is outside the body, but the immoral man sins against his own body. 19 Or do you not know that your body is a temple of the Holy Spirit who is in you, whom you have from God, and that you are not your own? 20 For you have been bought with a price: therefore glorify God in your body.

1 Corinthians

1 Corinthians 7

Teaching on Marriage

7 Now concerning the things about which you wrote, it is good for a man not to touch a woman. 2 But because of immoralities, each man is to have his own wife, and each woman is to have her own husband. 3 The husband must fulfill his duty to his wife, and likewise also the wife to her husband. 4 The wife does not have authority over her own body, but the husband does; and likewise also the husband does not have authority over his own body, but the wife does. 5 Stop depriving one another, except by agreement for a time, so that you may devote yourselves to prayer, and come together again so that Satan will not tempt you because of your lack of self-control. 6 But this I say by way of concession, not of command. 7 Yet I wish that all men were even as I myself am. However, each man has his own gift from God, one in this manner, and another in that.

8 But I say to the unmarried and to widows that it is good for them if they remain even as I. 9 But if they do not have self-control, let them marry; for it is better to marry than to burn with passion.

10 But to the married I give instructions, not I, but the Lord, that the wife should not leave her husband 11 (but if she does leave, she must remain unmarried, or else be reconciled to her husband), and that the husband should not divorce his wife.

12 But to the rest I say, not the Lord, that if any brother has a wife who is an unbeliever, and she consents to live with him, he must not divorce her. 13 And a woman who has an unbelieving husband, and he consents to live with her, she must not send her husband away.

14 For the unbelieving husband is sanctified through his wife, and the unbelieving wife is sanctified through her believing husband; for otherwise your children are unclean, but now they are holy.

15 Yet if the unbelieving one leaves, let him leave; the brother or the sister is not under bondage in such cases, but God has called us to peace.

16 For how do you know, O wife, whether you will save your husband? Or how do you know, O husband, whether you will save your wife?

17 Only, as the Lord has assigned to each one, as God has called each, in this manner let him walk. And so I direct in all the churches. 18 Was any man called when he was already circumcised? He is not to become uncircumcised. Has anyone been called in uncircumcision? He is not to be circumcised. 19 Circumcision is nothing, and uncircumcision is nothing, but what matters is the keeping of the commandments of God. 20 Each man must remain in that condition in which he was called.

21 Were you called while a slave? Do not worry about it; but if you are able also to become free, rather do that. 22 For he who was called in the Lord while a slave, is the Lord's freedman; likewise he who was called while free, is Christ's slave.

23 You were bought with a price; do not become slaves of men. 24 Brethren, each one is to remain with God in that condition in which he was called.

25 Now concerning virgins I have no command of the Lord, but I give an opinion as one who by the mercy of the Lord is trustworthy. 26 I think then that this is good in view of the present distress, that it is good for a man to remain as he is. 27 Are you bound to a wife? Do not seek to be released. Are you released from a wife? Do not seek a wife.

1 Corinthians

1 Corinthians 7

28 But if you marry, you have not sinned; and if a virgin marries, she has not sinned. Yet such will have trouble in this life, and I am trying to spare you. 29 But this I say, brethren, the time has been shortened, so that from now on those who have wives should be as though they had none; 30 and those who weep, as though they did not weep; and those who rejoice, as though they did not rejoice; and those who buy, as though they did not possess; 31 and those who use the world, as though they did not make full use of it; for the form of this world is passing away.

32 But I want you to be free from concern. One who is unmarried is concerned about the things of the Lord, how he may please the Lord; 33 but one who is married is concerned about the things of the world, how he may please his wife, 34 and his interests are divided. The woman who is unmarried, and the virgin, is concerned about the things of the Lord, that she may be holy both in body and spirit; but one who is married is concerned about the things of the world, how she may please her husband. 35 This I say for your own benefit; not to put a restraint upon you, but to promote what is appropriate and to secure undistracted devotion to the Lord.

36 But if any man thinks that he is acting unbecomingly toward his virgin daughter, if she is past her youth, and if it must be so, let him do what he wishes, he does not sin; let her marry. 37 But he who stands firm in his heart, being under no constraint, but has authority over his own will, and has decided this in his own heart, to keep his own virgin daughter, he will do well. 38 So then both he who gives his own virgin daughter in marriage does well, and he who does not give her in marriage will do better.

39 A wife is bound as long as her husband lives; but if her husband is dead, she is free to be married to whom she wishes, only in the Lord. 40 But in my opinion she is happier if she remains as she is; and I think that I also have the Spirit of God.

1 Corinthians

1 Corinthians 8

Take Care with Your Liberty

8 Now concerning things sacrificed to idols, we know that we all have knowledge. Knowledge makes arrogant, but love edifies. 2 If anyone supposes that he knows anything, he has not yet known as he ought to know; 3 but if anyone loves God, he is known by Him.

4 Therefore concerning the eating of things sacrificed to idols, we know that there is no such thing as an idol in the world, and that there is no God but one. 5 For even if there are so-called gods whether in heaven or on earth, as indeed there are many gods and many lords, 6 yet for us there is but one God, the Father, from whom are all things and we exist for Him; and one Lord, Jesus Christ, by whom are all things, and we exist through Him.

7 However not all men have this knowledge; but some, being accustomed to the idol until now, eat food as if it were sacrificed to an idol; and their conscience being weak is defiled. 8 But food will not commend us to God; we are neither the worse if we do not eat, nor the better if we do eat. 9 But take care that this liberty of yours does not somehow become a stumbling block to the weak. 10 For if someone sees you, who have knowledge, dining in an idol's temple, will not his conscience, if he is weak, be strengthened to eat things sacrificed to idols? 11 For through your knowledge he who is weak is ruined, the brother for whose sake Christ died. 12 And so, by sinning against the brethren and wounding their conscience when it is weak, you sin against Christ. 13 Therefore, if food causes my brother to stumble, I will never eat meat again, so that I will not cause my brother to stumble.

1 Corinthians

1 Corinthians 9

Paul's Use of Liberty

9 Am I not free? Am I not an apostle? Have I not seen Jesus our Lord? Are you not my work in the Lord? 2 If to others I am not an apostle, at least I am to you; for you are the seal of my apostleship in the Lord.
3 My defense to those who examine me is this:
4 Do we not have a right to eat and drink? 5 Do we not have a right to take along a believing wife, even as the rest of the apostles and the brothers of the Lord and Cephas? 6 Or do only Barnabas and I not have a right to refrain from working?
7 Who at any time serves as a soldier at his own expense? Who plants a vineyard and does not eat the fruit of it? Or who tends a flock and does not use the milk of the flock?
8 I am not speaking these things according to human judgment, am I? Or does not the Law also say these things? 9 For it is written in the Law of Moses, "You shall not muzzle the ox while he is threshing." God is not concerned about oxen, is He? 10 Or is He speaking altogether for our sake? Yes, for our sake it was written, because the plowman ought to plow in hope, and the thresher to thresh in hope of sharing the crops.
11 If we sowed spiritual things in you, is it too much if we reap material things from you? 12 If others share the right over you, do we not more? Nevertheless, we did not use this right, but we endure all things so that we will cause no hindrance to the gospel of Christ. 13 Do you not know that those who perform sacred services eat the food of the temple, and those who attend regularly to the altar have their share from the altar? 14 So also the Lord directed those who proclaim the gospel to get their living from the gospel.

15 But I have used none of these things. And I am not writing these things so that it will be done so in my case; for it would be better for me to die than have any man make my boast an empty one. 16 For if I preach the gospel, I have nothing to boast of, for I am under compulsion; for woe is me if I do not preach the gospel. 17 For if I do this voluntarily, I have a reward; but if against my will, I have a stewardship entrusted to me.
18 What then is my reward? That, when I preach the gospel, I may offer the gospel without charge, so as not to make full use of my right in the gospel.
19 For though I am free from all men, I have made myself a slave to all, so that I may win more. 20 To the Jews I became as a Jew, so that I might win Jews; to those who are under the Law, as under the Law though not being myself under the Law, so that I might win those who are under the Law; 21 to those who are without law, as without law, though not being without the law of God but under the law of Christ, so that I might win those who are without law. 22 To the weak I became weak, that I might win the weak; I have become all things to all men, so that I may by all means save some. 23 I do all things for the sake of the gospel, so that I may become a fellow partaker of it.
24 Do you not know that those who run in a race all run, but only one receives the prize? Run in such a way that you may win. 25 Everyone who competes in the games exercises self-control in all things. They then do it to receive a perishable wreath, but we an imperishable.
26 Therefore I run in such a way, as not without aim; I box in such a way, as not beating the air;
27 but I discipline my body and make it my slave, so that, after I have preached to others, I myself will not be disqualified.

1 Corinthians

1 Corinthians 10

Avoid Israel's Mistakes

10 For I do not want you to be unaware, brethren, that our fathers were all under the cloud and all passed through the sea; 2 and all were baptized into Moses in the cloud and in the sea; 3 and all ate the same spiritual food; 4 and all drank the same spiritual drink, for they were drinking from a spiritual rock which followed them; and the rock was Christ. 5 Nevertheless, with most of them God was not well-pleased; for they were laid low in the wilderness.

6 Now these things happened as examples for us, so that we would not crave evil things as they also craved. 7 Do not be idolaters, as some of them were; as it is written, "The people sat down to eat and drink, and stood up to play." 8 Nor let us act immorally, as some of them did, and twenty-three thousand fell in one day. 9 Nor let us try the Lord, as some of them did, and were destroyed by the serpents. 10 Nor grumble, as some of them did, and were destroyed by the destroyer. 11 Now these things happened to them as an example, and they were written for our instruction, upon whom the ends of the ages have come. 12 Therefore let him who thinks he stands take heed that he does not fall. 13 No temptation has overtaken you but such as is common to man; and God is faithful, who will not allow you to be tempted beyond what you are able, but with the temptation will provide the way of escape also, so that you will be able to endure it.

14 Therefore, my beloved, flee from idolatry. 15 I speak as to wise men; you judge what I say. 16 Is not the cup of blessing which we bless a sharing in the blood of Christ? Is not the bread which we break a sharing in the body of Christ? 17 Since there is one bread, we who are many are one body; for we all partake of the one bread.

18 Look at the nation Israel; are not those who eat the sacrifices sharers in the altar? 19 What do I mean then? That a thing sacrificed to idols is anything, or that an idol is anything? 20 No, but I say that the things which the Gentiles sacrifice, they sacrifice to demons and not to God; and I do not want you to become sharers in demons. 21 You cannot drink the cup of the Lord and the cup of demons; you cannot partake of the table of the Lord and the table of demons. 22 Or do we provoke the Lord to jealousy? We are not stronger than He, are we?

23 All things are lawful, but not all things are profitable. All things are lawful, but not all things edify. 24 Let no one seek his own good, but that of his neighbor. 25 Eat anything that is sold in the meat market without asking questions for conscience' sake; 26 for the earth is the Lord's, and all it contains. 27 If one of the unbelievers invites you and you want to go, eat anything that is set before you without asking questions for conscience' sake. 28 But if anyone says to you, "This is meat sacrificed to idols," do not eat it, for the sake of the one who informed you, and for conscience' sake; 29 I mean not your own conscience, but the other man's; for why is my freedom judged by another's conscience? 30 If I partake with thankfulness, why am I slandered concerning that for which I give thanks?

31 Whether, then, you eat or drink or whatever you do, do all to the glory of God. 32 Give no offense either to Jews or to Greeks or to the church of God; 33 just as I also please all men in all things, not seeking my own profit but the profit of the many, so that they may be saved.

1 Corinthians

1 Corinthians 11

11 Be imitators of me, just as I also am of Christ. 2 Now I praise you because you remember me in everything and hold firmly to the traditions, just as I delivered them to you. 3 But I want you to understand that Christ is the head of every man, and the man is the head of a woman, and God is the head of Christ. 4 Every man who has something on his head while praying or prophesying disgraces his head. 5 But every woman who has her head uncovered while praying or prophesying disgraces her head, for she is one and the same as the woman whose head is shaved. 6 For if a woman does not cover her head, let her also have her hair cut off; but if it is disgraceful for a woman to have her hair cut off or her head shaved, let her cover her head. 7 For a man ought not to have his head covered, since he is the image and glory of God; but the woman is the glory of man. 8 For man does not originate from woman, but woman from man; 9 for indeed man was not created for the woman's sake, but woman for the man's sake. 10 Therefore the woman ought to have a symbol of authority on her head, because of the angels. 11 However, in the Lord, neither is woman independent of man, nor is man independent of woman. 12 For as the woman originates from the man, so also the man has his birth through the woman; and all things originate from God. 13 Judge for yourselves: is it proper for a woman to pray to God with her head uncovered? 14 Does not even nature itself teach you that if a man has long hair, it is a dishonor to him, 15 but if a woman has long hair, it is a glory to her? For her hair is given to her for a covering. 16 But if one is inclined to be contentious, we have no other practice, nor have the churches of God.

17 But in giving this instruction, I do not praise you, because you come together not for the better but for the worse. 18 For, in the first place, when you come together as a church, I hear that divisions exist among you; and in part I believe it.

19 For there must also be factions among you, so that those who are approved may become evident among you. 20 Therefore when you meet together, it is not to eat the Lord's Supper, 21 for in your eating each one takes his own supper first; and one is hungry and another is drunk. 22 What! Do you not have houses in which to eat and drink? Or do you despise the church of God and shame those who have nothing? What shall I say to you? Shall I praise you? In this I will not praise you.

The Lord's Supper

23 For I received from the Lord that which I also delivered to you, that the Lord Jesus in the night in which He was betrayed took bread; 24 and when He had given thanks, He broke it and said, "This is My body, which is for you; do this in remembrance of Me." 25 In the same way He took the cup also after supper, saying, "This cup is the new covenant in My blood; do this, as often as you drink it, in remembrance of Me." 26 For as often as you eat this bread and drink the cup, you proclaim the Lord's death until He comes. 27 Therefore whoever eats the bread or drinks the cup of the Lord in an unworthy manner, shall be guilty of the body and the blood of the Lord. 28 But a man must examine himself, and in so doing he is to eat of the bread and drink of the cup. 29 For he who eats and drinks, eats and drinks judgment to himself if he does not judge the body rightly. 30 For this reason many among you are weak and sick, and a number sleep. 31 But if we judged ourselves rightly, we would not be judged. 32 But when we are judged, we are disciplined by the Lord so that we will not be condemned along with the world.

33 So then, my brethren, when you come together to eat, wait for one another. 34 If anyone is hungry, let him eat at home, so that you will not come together for judgment. The remaining matters I will arrange when I come.

1 Corinthians

1 Corinthians 12

The Use of Spiritual Gifts

12 Now concerning spiritual gifts, brethren, I do not want you to be unaware. 2 You know that when you were pagans, you were led astray to the mute idols, however you were led.
3 Therefore I make known to you that no one speaking by the Spirit of God says, "Jesus is accursed"; and no one can say, "Jesus is Lord," except by the Holy Spirit.
4 Now there are varieties of gifts, but the same Spirit. 5 And there are varieties of ministries, and the same Lord. 6 There are varieties of effects, but the same God who works all things in all persons. 7 But to each one is given the manifestation of the Spirit for the common good. 8 For to one is given the word of wisdom through the Spirit, and to another the word of knowledge according to the same Spirit; 9 to another faith by the same Spirit, and to another gifts of healing by the one Spirit, 10 and to another the effecting of miracles, and to another prophecy, and to another the distinguishing of spirits, to another various kinds of tongues, and to another the interpretation of tongues. 11 But one and the same Spirit works all these things, distributing to each one individually just as He wills.
12 For even as the body is one and yet has many members, and all the members of the body, though they are many, are one body, so also is Christ. 13 For by one Spirit we were all baptized into one body, whether Jews or Greeks, whether slaves or free, and we were all made to drink of one Spirit.
14 For the body is not one member, but many. 15 If the foot says, "Because I am not a hand, I am not a part of the body," it is not for this reason any the less a part of the body. 16 And if the ear says, "Because I am not an eye, I am not a part of the body," it is not for this reason any the less a part of the body. 17 If the whole body were an eye, where would the hearing be? If the whole were hearing, where would the sense of smell be?

18 But now God has placed the members, each one of them, in the body, just as He desired. 19 If they were all one member, where would the body be? 20 But now there are many members, but one body. 21 And the eye cannot say to the hand, "I have no need of you"; or again the head to the feet, "I have no need of you." 22 On the contrary, it is much truer that the members of the body which seem to be weaker are necessary; 23 and those members of the body which we deem less honorable, on these we bestow more abundant honor, and our less presentable members become much more presentable, 24 whereas our more presentable members have no need of it. But God has so composed the body, giving more abundant honor to that member which lacked, 25 so that there may be no division in the body, but that the members may have the same care for one another. 26 And if one member suffers, all the members suffer with it; if one member is honored, all the members rejoice with it.
27 Now you are Christ's body, and individually members of it. 28 And God has appointed in the church, first apostles, second prophets, third teachers, then miracles, then gifts of healings, helps, administrations, various kinds of tongues. 29 All are not apostles, are they? All are not prophets, are they? All are not teachers, are they? All are not workers of miracles, are they? 30 All do not have gifts of healings, do they? All do not speak with tongues, do they? All do not interpret, do they? 31 But earnestly desire the greater gifts. And I show you a still more excellent way.

1 Corinthians

1 Corinthians 13

The Excellence of Love

13 If I speak with the tongues of men and of angels, but do not have love, I have become a noisy gong or a clanging cymbal. 2 If I have the gift of prophecy, and know all mysteries and all knowledge; and if I have all faith, so as to remove mountains, but do not have love, I am nothing. 3 And if I give all my possessions to feed the poor, and if I surrender my body to be burned, but do not have love, it profits me nothing. 4 Love is patient, love is kind and is not jealous; love does not brag and is not arrogant, 5 does not act unbecomingly; it does not seek its own, is not provoked, does not take into account a wrong suffered, 6 does not rejoice in unrighteousness, but rejoices with the truth; 7 bears all things, believes all things, hopes all things, endures all things.
8 Love never fails; but if there are gifts of prophecy, they will be done away; if there are tongues, they will cease; if there is knowledge, it will be done away. 9 For we know in part and we prophesy in part; 10 but when the perfect comes, the partial will be done away. 11 When I was a child, I used to speak like a child, think like a child, reason like a child; when I became a man, I did away with childish things. 12 For now we see in a mirror dimly, but then face to face; now I know in part, but then I will know fully just as I also have been fully known. 13 But now faith, hope, love, abide these three; but the greatest of these is love.

1 Corinthians

1 Corinthians 14

Prophecy a Superior Gift

14 Pursue love, yet desire earnestly spiritual gifts, but especially that you may prophesy. 2 For one who speaks in a tongue does not speak to men but to God; for no one understands, but in his spirit he speaks mysteries. 3 But one who prophesies speaks to men for edification and exhortation and consolation. 4 One who speaks in a tongue edifies himself; but one who prophesies edifies the church. 5 Now I wish that you all spoke in tongues, but even more that you would prophesy; and greater is one who prophesies than one who speaks in tongues, unless he interprets, so that the church may receive edifying.

6 But now, brethren, if I come to you speaking in tongues, what will I profit you unless I speak to you either by way of revelation or of knowledge or of prophecy or of teaching? 7 Yet even lifeless things, either flute or harp, in producing a sound, if they do not produce a distinction in the tones, how will it be known what is played on the flute or on the harp? 8 For if the bugle produces an indistinct sound, who will prepare himself for battle? 9 So also you, unless you utter by the tongue speech that is clear, how will it be known what is spoken? For you will be speaking into the air. 10 There are, perhaps, a great many kinds of languages in the world, and no kind is without meaning. 11 If then I do not know the meaning of the language, I will be to the one who speaks a barbarian, and the one who speaks will be a barbarian to me. 12 So also you, since you are zealous of spiritual gifts, seek to abound for the edification of the church.

13 Therefore let one who speaks in a tongue pray that he may interpret. 14 For if I pray in a tongue, my spirit prays, but my mind is unfruitful. 15 What is the outcome then? I will pray with the spirit and I will pray with the mind also; I will sing with the spirit and I will sing with the mind also.

16 Otherwise if you bless in the spirit only, how will the one who fills the place of the ungifted say the "Amen" at your giving of thanks, since he does not know what you are saying? 17 For you are giving thanks well enough, but the other person is not edified. 18 I thank God, I speak in tongues more than you all; 19 however, in the church I desire to speak five words with my mind so that I may instruct others also, rather than ten thousand words in a tongue.

Instruction for the Church

20 Brethren, do not be children in your thinking; yet in evil be infants, but in your thinking be mature. 21 In the Law it is written, "By men of strange tongues and by the lips of strangers I will speak to this people, and even so they will not listen to Me," says the Lord. 22 So then tongues are for a sign, not to those who believe but to unbelievers; but prophecy is for a sign, not to unbelievers but to those who believe. 23 Therefore if the whole church assembles together and all speak in tongues, and ungifted men or unbelievers enter, will they not say that you are mad? 24 But if all prophesy, and an unbeliever or an ungifted man enters, he is convicted by all, he is called to account by all; 25 the secrets of his heart are disclosed; and so he will fall on his face and worship God, declaring that God is certainly among you.

1 Corinthians

1 Corinthians 14

26 What is the outcome then, brethren? When you assemble, each one has a psalm, has a teaching, has a revelation, has a tongue, has an interpretation. Let all things be done for edification. 27 If anyone speaks in a tongue, it should be by two or at the most three, and each in turn, and one must interpret; 28 but if there is no interpreter, he must keep silent in the church; and let him speak to himself and to God. 29 Let two or three prophets speak, and let the others pass judgment. 30 But if a revelation is made to another who is seated, the first one must keep silent. 31 For you can all prophesy one by one, so that all may learn and all may be exhorted; 32 and the spirits of prophets are subject to prophets; 33 for God is not a God of confusion but of peace, as in all the churches of the saints. 34 The women are to keep silent in the churches; for they are not permitted to speak, but are to subject themselves, just as the Law also says. 35 If they desire to learn anything, let them ask their own husbands at home; for it is improper for a woman to speak in church. 36 Was it from you that the word of God first went forth? Or has it come to you only?

37 If anyone thinks he is a prophet or spiritual, let him recognize that the things which I write to you are the Lord's commandment. 38 But if anyone does not recognize this, he is not recognized.

39 Therefore, my brethren, desire earnestly to prophesy, and do not forbid to speak in tongues. 40 But all things must be done properly and in an orderly manner.

1 Corinthians

1 Corinthians 15

The Fact of Christ's Resurrection

15 Now I make known to you, brethren, the gospel which I preached to you, which also you received, in which also you stand, 2 by which also you are saved, if you hold fast the word which I preached to you, unless you believed in vain.
3 For I delivered to you as of first importance what I also received, that Christ died for our sins according to the Scriptures, 4 and that He was buried, and that He was raised on the third day according to the Scriptures, 5 and that He appeared to Cephas, then to the twelve. 6 After that He appeared to more than five hundred brethren at one time, most of whom remain until now, but some have fallen asleep; 7 then He appeared to James, then to all the apostles; 8 and last of all, as to one untimely born, He appeared to me also. 9 For I am the least of the apostles, and not fit to be called an apostle, because I persecuted the church of God. 10 But by the grace of God I am what I am, and His grace toward me did not prove vain; but I labored even more than all of them, yet not I, but the grace of God with me. 11 Whether then it was I or they, so we preach and so you believed.
12 Now if Christ is preached, that He has been raised from the dead, how do some among you say that there is no resurrection of the dead?
13 But if there is no resurrection of the dead, not even Christ has been raised; 14 and if Christ has not been raised, then our preaching is vain, your faith also is vain. 15 Moreover we are even found to be false witnesses of God, because we testified against God that He raised Christ, whom He did not raise, if in fact the dead are not raised. 16 For if the dead are not raised, not even Christ has been raised; 17 and if Christ has not been raised, your faith is worthless; you are still in your sins.
18 Then those also who have fallen asleep in Christ have perished. 19 If we have hoped in Christ in this life only, we are of all men most to be pitied.

1 Corinthians

1 Corinthians 16

13 Be on the alert, stand firm in the faith, act like men, be strong. 14 Let all that you do be done in love.

Pneumatology
Notes

Summative assessment
Position paper notes

What I believe:

Why do I believe it?

What difference will it make in my life?

Anthropology

Doctrine & Apologetics
INVITED TO GO AND TEACH

Unit Essential Questions

1. How does theological anthropology define man's need for God?

2. What is our relationship to the Law?

3. What is our relationship to grace?

4. What is sanctification, and how does God change us?

Reading

Know What You Believe, Chapter 5

Unit Learning Assessments

Summative:

Position paper

Daily Learning Plan

7.1 What is the doctrine of the *imago Dei?*
What are the theological implications of cloning?

7.2 What is the doctrine of total depravity?

7.3 What is our relation to the Law?
What is our relation to grace?

7.4 What are the implications of anthropology and total depravity to salvation?
What are the implications of anthropology and total depravity to sanctification?

Anthropology
YouTube Friday

Doctrine & Apologetics

Anthropology
Reading notes

Know What You Believe, Chapter 5: Man and Sin

Definitions:

- Total depravity

1. Summarize Augustine's view of the Fall in a sentence or two.

2. How does theological anthropology define man's need for God?

3. What is our relationship to the Law?

4. What is our relationship to grace?

5. What is sanctification, and how does God change us?

Anthropology
Mini Project

Two friends from school—a male and female—approach you in confidence and share with you that they have been sexually active together. As a result, she is pregnant and considering an abortion. How would you counsel her, and why? Use Scripture to back up your answer, however, you cannot use "thou shalt not kill."

Two friends have a baby who dies tragically. You go to the hospital to visit them, and through their tears, one of them confesses to you that they don't know how this tragedy could have happened when they both have loved God their whole lives and kept themselves pure prior to marriage. Now they feel like God has turned His back on them, and they wonder whether they will see their baby in heaven.

How would you use Scripture to counsel them?

107

Summative assessment
Position paper notes

What I believe:

Why do I believe it?

What difference will it make in my life?

Soteriology

Doctrine & Apologetics

INVITED TO GO AND TEACH

Unit Essential Questions

1. What is the gospel?

2. What does it mean to be saved?

Reading

Know Why You Believe, Chapter 7

Know What You Believe, Chapter 8

Unit Learning Assessments

Summative:

Position paper

Daily Learning Plan

8.1   What is the gospel?

8.2   What are the elements of saving faith?

What are the results of saving faith?

8.3   What is the theological tension between monergism and synergism?

What are the theological implications of monergistic and synergistic beliefs?

8.4   Is there a Biblical apologetic for an age of accountability?

Soteriology
YouTube Friday

Soteriology

Reading notes

Know What You Believe, Chapter 7: Salvation

Explain the terms "election," "predestination," and "foreknowledge" as they relate to salvation:

- Election

- Predestination

- Foreknowledge

Explain the terms and the implications of mongergism and synergism:

- Monergism

- Synergism

Essential questions:

1. What are the elements of saving faith?

2. What are the results of saving faith?

Soteriology
Reading notes

Know Why You Believe, Chapter 8: Are miracles possible?

1. What do we mean by "natural law" or "the laws of nature" (p. 102)?

2. Is God ruled by the laws of nature? Explain.

3. What is the relationship between the laws of nature and miracles (pp. 104-105)?

4. What two purposes did biblical miracles fulfill (pp.105-106)?

5. How can you tell the difference between biblical miracles and "pagan" miracles (p. 109)?

Romans

Romans 8

Deliverance from Bondage

8 Therefore there is now no condemnation for those who are in Christ Jesus. 2 For the law of the Spirit of life in Christ Jesus has set you free from the law of sin and of death. 3 For what the Law could not do, weak as it was through the flesh, God did: sending His own Son in the likeness of sinful flesh and as an offering for sin, He condemned sin in the flesh, 4 so that the requirement of the Law might be fulfilled in us, who do not walk according to the flesh but according to the Spirit. 5 For those who are according to the flesh set their minds on the things of the flesh, but those who are according to the Spirit, the things of the Spirit. 6 For the mind set on the flesh is death, but the mind set on the Spirit is life and peace, 7 because the mind set on the flesh is hostile toward God; for it does not subject itself to the law of God, for it is not even able to do so, 8 and those who are in the flesh cannot please God.

9 However, you are not in the flesh but in the Spirit, if indeed the Spirit of God dwells in you. But if anyone does not have the Spirit of Christ, he does not belong to Him. 10 If Christ is in you, though the body is dead because of sin, yet the spirit is alive because of righteousness. 11 But if the Spirit of Him who raised Jesus from the dead dwells in you, He who raised Christ Jesus from the dead will also give life to your mortal bodies through His Spirit who dwells in you.

12 So then, brethren, we are under obligation, not to the flesh, to live according to the flesh— 13 for if you are living according to the flesh, you must die; but if by the Spirit you are putting to death the deeds of the body, you will live.

14 For all who are being led by the Spirit of God, these are sons of God. 15 For you have not received a spirit of slavery leading to fear again, but you have received a spirit of adoption as sons by which we cry out, "Abba! Father!" 16 The Spirit Himself testifies with our spirit that we are children of God, 17 and if children, heirs also, heirs of God and fellow heirs with Christ, if indeed we suffer with Him so that we may also be glorified with Him.

18 For I consider that the sufferings of this present time are not worthy to be compared with the glory that is to be revealed to us. 19 For the anxious longing of the creation waits eagerly for the revealing of the sons of God. 20 For the creation was subjected to futility, not willingly, but because of Him who subjected it, in hope 21 that the creation itself also will be set free from its slavery to corruption into the freedom of the glory of the children of God. 22 For we know that the whole creation groans and suffers the pains of childbirth together until now. 23 And not only this, but also we ourselves, having the first fruits of the Spirit, even we ourselves groan within ourselves, waiting eagerly for our adoption as sons, the redemption of our body. 24 For in hope we have been saved, but hope that is seen is not hope; for who hopes for what he already sees? 25 But if we hope for what we do not see, with perseverance we wait eagerly for it.

Romans
Romans 8-9

26 In the same way the Spirit also helps our weakness; for we do not know how to pray as we should, but the Spirit Himself intercedes for us with groanings too deep for words; 27 and He who searches the hearts knows what the mind of the Spirit is, because He intercedes for the saints according to the will of God.

28 And we know that God causes all things to work together for good to those who love God, to those who are called according to His purpose. 29 For those whom He foreknew, He also predestined to become conformed to the image of His Son, so that He would be the firstborn among many brethren; 30 and these whom He predestined, He also called; and these whom He called, He also justified; and these whom He justified, He also glorified.

31 What then shall we say to these things? If God is for us, who is against us? 32 He who did not spare His own Son, but delivered Him over for us all, how will He not also with Him freely give us all things? 33 Who will bring a charge against God's elect? God is the one who justifies; 34 who is the one who condemns? Christ Jesus is He who died, yes, rather who was raised, who is at the right hand of God, who also intercedes for us.

35 Who will separate us from the love of Christ? Will tribulation, or distress, or persecution, or famine, or nakedness, or peril, or sword? 36 Just as it is written,

> "For Your sake we are being put to death all day long; We were considered as sheep to be slaughtered."

37 But in all these things we overwhelmingly conquer through Him who loved us. 38 For I am convinced that neither death, nor life, nor angels, nor principalities, nor things present, nor things to come, nor powers, 39 nor height, nor depth, nor any other created thing, will be able to separate us from the love of God, which is in Christ Jesus our Lord.

Romans

Romans 9

Solicitude for Israel

9 I am telling the truth in Christ, I am not lying, my conscience testifies with me in the Holy Spirit, 2 that I have great sorrow and unceasing grief in my heart. 3 For I could wish that I myself were accursed, separated from Christ for the sake of my brethren, my kinsmen according to the flesh, 4 who are Israelites, to whom belongs the adoption as sons, and the glory and the covenants and the giving of the Law and the temple service and the promises, 5 whose are the fathers, and from whom is the Christ according to the flesh, who is over all, God blessed forever. Amen.

6 But it is not as though the word of God has failed. For they are not all Israel who are descended from Israel; 7 nor are they all children because they are Abraham's descendants, but: "through Isaac your descendants will be named."

8 That is, it is not the children of the flesh who are children of God, but the children of the promise are regarded as descendants. 9 For this is the word of promise: "At this time I will come, and Sarah shall have a son." 10 And not only this, but there was Rebekah also, when she had conceived twins by one man, our father Isaac;

11 for though the twins were not yet born and had not done anything good or bad, so that God's purpose according to His choice would stand, not because of works but because of Him who calls, 12 it was said to her, "The older will serve the younger." 13 Just as it is written, "Jacob I loved, but Esau I hated."

14 What shall we say then? There is no injustice with God, is there? May it never be!

15 For He says to Moses, "I will have mercy on whom I have mercy, and I will have compassion on whom I have compassion." 16 So then it does not depend on the man who wills or the man who runs, but on God who has mercy. 17 For the Scripture says to Pharaoh, "For this very purpose I raised you up, to demonstrate My power in you, and that My name might be proclaimed throughout the whole earth." 18 So then He has mercy on whom He desires, and He hardens whom He desires.

19 You will say to me then, "Why does He still find fault? For who resists His will?"

20 On the contrary, who are you, O man, who answers back to God? The thing molded will not say to the molder, "Why did you make me like this," will it?

21 Or does not the potter have a right over the clay, to make from the same lump one vessel for honorable use and another for common use?

22 What if God, although willing to demonstrate His wrath and to make His power known, endured with much patience vessels of wrath prepared for destruction? 23 And He did so to make known the riches of His glory upon vessels of mercy, which He prepared beforehand for glory, 24 even us, whom He also called, not from among Jews only, but also from among Gentiles.

25 As He says also in Hosea,

> "I will call those who were not My people, 'My people,' And her who was not beloved, 'beloved.'"
> 26 "And it shall be that in the place where it was said to them, 'you are not My people,' There they shall be called sons of the living God."

Romans
Romans 9

27 Isaiah cries out concerning Israel, "Though the number of the sons of Israel be like the sand of the sea, it is the remnant that will be saved; 28 for the Lord will execute His word on the earth, thoroughly and quickly." 29 And just as Isaiah foretold, "Unless the Lord of Sabaoth had left to us a posterity, We would have become like Sodom, and would have resembled Gomorrah."

30 What shall we say then? That Gentiles, who did not pursue righteousness, attained righteousness, even the righteousness which is by faith; 31 but Israel, pursuing a law of righteousness, did not arrive at that law.

32 Why?

Because they did not pursue it by faith, but as though it were by works. They stumbled over the stumbling stone, 33 just as it is written,

> "Behold, I lay in Zion a stone of stumbling and a rock of offense, And he who believes in Him will not be disappointed."

Romans

Romans 10-11:6

10 Brethren, my heart's desire and my prayer to God for them is for their salvation. 2 For I testify about them that they have a zeal for God, but not in accordance with knowledge. 3 For not knowing about God's righteousness and seeking to establish their own, they did not subject themselves to the righteousness of God. 4 For Christ is the end of the law for righteousness to everyone who believes.

5 For Moses writes that the man who practices the righteousness which is based on law shall live by that righteousness. 6 But the righteousness based on faith speaks as follows: "Do not say in your heart, 'Who will ascend into heaven?' (that is, to bring Christ down), 7 or 'Who will descend into the abyss?' (that is, to bring Christ up from the dead)."

8 But what does it say? "The word is near you, in your mouth and in your heart"—that is, the word of faith which we are preaching, 9 that if you confess with your mouth Jesus as Lord, and believe in your heart that God raised Him from the dead, you will be saved; 10 for with the heart a person believes, resulting in righteousness, and with the mouth he confesses, resulting in salvation. 11 For the Scripture says, "Whoever believes in Him will not be disappointed."

12 For there is no distinction between Jew and Greek; for the same Lord is Lord of all, abounding in riches for all who call on Him; 13 for "Whoever will call on the name of the Lord will be saved."

14 How then will they call on Him in whom they have not believed? How will they believe in Him whom they have not heard? And how will they hear without a preacher? 15 How will they preach unless they are sent? Just as it is written, "How beautiful are the feet of those who bring good news of good things!"

16 However, they did not all heed the good news; for Isaiah says, "Lord, who has believed our report?" 17 So faith comes from hearing, and hearing by the word of Christ.

18 But I say, surely they have never heard, have they? Indeed they have; "Their voice has gone out into all the earth, And their words to the ends of the world."

19 But I say, surely Israel did not know, did they?

First Moses says, "I will make you jealous by that which is not a nation, By a nation without understanding will I anger you."

20 And Isaiah is very bold and says, "I was found by those who did not seek Me, I became manifest to those who did not ask for Me."

21 But as for Israel He says, "All the day long I have stretched out My hands to a disobedient and obstinate people."

11:1 I say then, God has not rejected His people, has He? May it never be! For I too am an Israelite, a descendant of Abraham, of the tribe of Benjamin.

2 God has not rejected His people whom He foreknew. Or do you not know what the Scripture says in the passage about Elijah, how he pleads with God against Israel? 3 "Lord, they have killed Your prophets, they have torn down Your altars, and I alone am left, and they are seeking my life."

4 But what is the divine response to him? "I have kept for Myself seven thousand men who have not bowed the knee to Baal." 5 In the same way then, there has also come to be at the present time a remnant according to God's gracious choice. 6 But if it is by grace, it is no longer on the basis of works, otherwise grace is no longer grace.

Soteriology
notes

119

Summative assessment
Position paper notes

What I believe:

Why do I believe it?

What difference will it make in my life?

Angelology

Doctrine & Apologetics

INVITED TO GO AND TEACH

Unit Essential Questions

1. What is our relationship with angels?

2. Who is Satan, and what is his role in God's story?

Reading

Know What You Believe, Chapter 8

Unit Learning Assessments

Summative:

Position paper

Daily Learning Plan

9.1 Who is Satan, and what is his role in God's story? What is his role in my story?

9.2 What is our relationship with angels?

9.3 What is spiritual warfare?

9.4 How does Ephesians 6 apply to my daily life?

Angelology
YouTube Friday

123

Angelology

Reading notes

Know What You Believe, Chapter 8: Angels, Satan, and Demons

1. Describe five attributes of angels. Give a specific instance when the media has strayed from these biblical characteristics.

    •

    •

    •

    •

    •

2. Describe three facets of angelic activity:

    •

    •

    •

3. List and describe two common misconceptions about angels.

    •

    •

4. List four biblical truths about Satan.

    •

    •

    •

    •

Angelology
notes

125

Summative assessment
Position paper notes

What I believe:

Why do I believe it?

What difference will it make in my life?

Ecclesiology

Doctrine & Apologetics
INVITED TO GO AND TEACH

Unit Essential Questions

1. What is the church?

2. What are the qualifications of church leaders?

3. What is our relationship to the church as young adults?

Reading

Know What You Believe, Chapter 9

Unit Learning Assessments

Summative:

Position paper

Daily Learning Plan

10.1   What is the church?

10.2   What are the biblical roles and qualifications for church leaders?

10.3   Did Paul think women were human?

10.4   What are the implications of God's blueprint for the church?

Ecclesiology
Reflection

Examine your own view of church.

- Do you see church more as a building or as people gathered together?

- Why are you part of the church?

- What are you gaining spiritually, and how are you serving in your church?

- What changes do you need to make?

129

Ecclesiology

Reading notes

Know What You Believe, Chapter 9: The Church

Definitions:

- How does the word *ekklesia* describe the church?

  By calling those who have been called out to Jesus Christ

- How do the following metaphors describe the church?

  The body of Christ (1 Cor. 12:12-31)

  By knowing that the Body of Christ is made up of diverse and unique loving people

  The building of Christ (1 Peter 2:5, 1 Cor. 6:19-20)

  The home of Christ believers

  The bride of Christ (Eph. 5:25-27, 31-32; 2 Cor. 11:2; Rev. 19:7, 22:17)

  The love of Christ being spread throughout the body of Christ.

Ecclesiology
Notes

131

Summative assessment
Position paper notes

What I believe:

Why do I believe it?

What difference will it make in my life?

Eschatology

Doctrine & Apologetics
INVITED TO GO AND TEACH

Unit Essential Questions

1. How does our view of Scripture impact our view of the end times?

2. What difference should our eschatological beliefs have on our daily lives?

Reading

Know What You Believe, Chapter 10

Unit Learning Assessments

Summative:

Position paper

Daily Learning Plan

11.1 How does our view of Scripture impact our view of the end times?

11.2 What is the significance of recent historical events on biblical prophecy?

11.3 What are the implications of differing eschatological views?

11.4 Are we living in the end times?

Eschatology
Reading notes

Know What You Believe, Chapter 10: Things to come

Definitions:

- Tribulation

- Rapture

- Pretribulation

- Midtribulation

- Amillennialism

1. What are the differences between premillennialism and amillennialism

2. What happens to believers' bodies when they are resurrected?

3. How would you explain this sad fact? "There is no biblical evidence for believing in the final restoration of
    the lost or in the universal salvation of all men."

- How can this reality encourage you to witness to unbelievers?

Ezekiel

Ezekiel 37

Vision of the Valley of Dry Bones

37 The hand of the Lord was upon me, and He brought me out by the Spirit of the Lord and set me down in the middle of the valley; and it was full of bones. 2 He caused me to pass among them round about, and behold, there were very many on the surface of the valley; and lo, they were very dry. 3 He said to me, "Son of man, can these bones live?"

And I answered, "O Lord God, You know." 4 Again He said to me, "Prophesy over these bones and say to them, 'O dry bones, hear the word of the Lord.' 5 Thus says the Lord God to these bones, 'Behold, I will cause breath to enter you that you may come to life. 6 I will put sinews on you, make flesh grow back on you, cover you with skin and put breath in you that you may come alive; and you will know that I am the Lord.'"

7 So I prophesied as I was commanded; and as I prophesied, there was a noise, and behold, a rattling; and the bones came together, bone to its bone. 8 And I looked, and behold, sinews were on them, and flesh grew and skin covered them; but there was no breath in them.

9 Then He said to me, "Prophesy to the breath, prophesy, son of man, and say to the breath, 'Thus says the Lord God, "Come from the four winds, O breath, and breathe on these slain, that they come to life."'"

10 So I prophesied as He commanded me, and the breath came into them, and they came to life and stood on their feet, an exceedingly great army.

The Vision Explained

11 Then He said to me, "Son of man, these bones are the whole house of Israel; behold, they say, 'Our bones are dried up and our hope has perished. We are completely cut off.' 12 Therefore prophesy and say to them, 'Thus says the Lord God, "Behold, I will open your graves and cause you to come up out of your graves, My people; and I will bring you into the land of Israel.

13 Then you will know that I am the Lord, when I have opened your graves and caused you to come up out of your graves, My people. 14 I will put My Spirit within you and you will come to life, and I will place you on your own land. Then you will know that I, the Lord, have spoken and done it," declares the Lord.'"

15 The word of the Lord came again to me saying, 16 "And you, son of man, take for yourself one stick and write on it, 'For Judah and for the sons of Israel, his companions'; then take another stick and write on it, 'For Joseph, the stick of Ephraim and all the house of Israel, his companions.' 17 Then join them for yourself one to another into one stick, that they may become one in your hand. 18 When the sons of your people speak to you saying, 'Will you not declare to us what you mean by these?' 19 say to them, 'Thus says the Lord God, "Behold, I will take the stick of Joseph, which is in the hand of Ephraim, and the tribes of Israel, his companions; and I will put them with it, with the stick of Judah, and make them one stick, and they will be one in My hand."' 20 The sticks on which you write will be in your hand before their eyes. 21 Say to them, 'Thus says the Lord God, "Behold, I will take the sons of Israel from among the nations where they have gone, and I will gather them from every side and bring them into their own land; 22 and I will make them one nation in the land, on the mountains of Israel; and one king will be king for all of them; and they will no longer be two nations and no longer be divided into two kingdoms.

Ezekiel
Ezekiel 37

23 They will no longer defile themselves with their idols, or with their detestable things, or with any of their transgressions; but I will deliver them from all their dwelling places in which they have sinned, and will cleanse them. And they will be My people, and I will be their God.

The Davidic Kingdom

24 "My servant David will be king over them, and they will all have one shepherd; and they will walk in My ordinances and keep My statutes and observe them.

25 They will live on the land that I gave to Jacob My servant, in which your fathers lived; and they will live on it, they, and their sons and their sons' sons, forever; and David My servant will be their prince forever. 26 I will make a covenant of peace with them; it will be an everlasting covenant with them. And I will place them and multiply them, and will set My sanctuary in their midst forever.

27 My dwelling place also will be with them; and I will be their God, and they will be My people.

28 And the nations will know that I am the Lord who sanctifies Israel, when My sanctuary is in their midst forever.""""

137

Ezekiel

Ezekiel 38

Prophecy about Gog and Future Invasion of Israel

38 And the word of the Lord came to me saying, 2 "Son of man, set your face toward Gog of the land of Magog, the prince of Rosh, Meshech and Tubal, and prophesy against him 3 and say, 'Thus says the Lord God, "Behold, I am against you, O Gog, prince of Rosh, Meshech and Tubal.

4 I will turn you about and put hooks into your jaws, and I will bring you out, and all your army, horses and horsemen, all of them splendidly attired, a great company with buckler and shield, all of them wielding swords; 5 Persia, Ethiopia and Put with them, all of them with shield and helmet; 6 Gomer with all its troops; Beth-togarmah from the remote parts of the north with all its troops —many peoples with you.

7 "Be prepared, and prepare yourself, you and all your companies that are assembled about you, and be a guard for them. 8 After many days you will be summoned; in the latter years you will come into the land that is restored from the sword, whose inhabitants have been gathered from many nations to the mountains of Israel which had been a continual waste; but its people were brought out from the nations, and they are living securely, all of them. 9 You will go up, you will come like a storm; you will be like a cloud covering the land, you and all your troops, and many peoples with you."

10 'Thus says the Lord God, "It will come about on that day, that thoughts will come into your mind and you will devise an evil plan, 11 and you will say, 'I will go up against the land of unwalled villages. I will go against those who are at rest, that live securely, all of them living without walls and having no bars or gates, 12 to capture spoil and to seize plunder, to turn your hand against the waste places which are now inhabited, and against the people who are gathered from the nations, who have acquired cattle and goods, who live at the center of the world.'

Ezekiel

Ezekiel 38

Prophecy about Gog and Future Invasion of Israel

13 Sheba and Dedan and the merchants of Tarshish with all its villages will say to you, 'Have you come to capture spoil? Have you assembled your company to seize plunder, to carry away silver and gold, to take away cattle and goods, to capture great spoil?'"

14 "Therefore prophesy, son of man, and say to Gog, 'Thus says the Lord God, "On that day when My people Israel are living securely, will you not know it? 15 You will come from your place out of the remote parts of the north, you and many peoples with you, all of them riding on horses, a great assembly and a mighty army; 16 and you will come up against My people Israel like a cloud to cover the land. It shall come about in the last days that I will bring you against My land, so that the nations may know Me when I am sanctified through you before their eyes, O Gog."

17 'Thus says the Lord God, "Are you the one of whom I spoke in former days through My servants the prophets of Israel, who prophesied in those days for many years that I would bring you against them?

18 It will come about on that day, when Gog comes against the land of Israel," declares the Lord God, "that My fury will mount up in My anger. 19 In My zeal and in My blazing wrath I declare that on that day there will surely be a great earthquake in the land of Israel.

20 The fish of the sea, the birds of the heavens, the beasts of the field, all the creeping things that creep on the earth, and all the men who are on the face of the earth will shake at My presence; the mountains also will be thrown down, the steep pathways will collapse and every wall will fall to the ground.

21 I will call for a sword against him on all My mountains," declares the Lord God. "Every man's sword will be against his brother. 22 With pestilence and with blood I will enter into judgment with him; and I will rain on him and on his troops, and on the many peoples who are with him, a torrential rain, with hailstones, fire and brimstone. 23 I will magnify Myself, sanctify Myself, and make Myself known in the sight of many nations; and they will know that I am the Lord.'"

139

Ezekiel

Ezekiel 39

Prophecy against Gog—Invaders Destroyed

39 "And you, son of man, prophesy against Gog and say, 'Thus says the Lord God, "Behold, I am against you, O Gog, prince of Rosh, Meshech and Tubal; 2 and I will turn you around, drive you on, take you up from the remotest parts of the north and bring you against the mountains of Israel.

3 I will strike your bow from your left hand and dash down your arrows from your right hand.

4 You will fall on the mountains of Israel, you and all your troops and the peoples who are with you; I will give you as food to every kind of predatory bird and beast of the field. 5 You will fall on the open field; for it is I who have spoken," declares the Lord God.

6 "And I will send fire upon Magog and those who inhabit the coastlands in safety; and they will know that I am the Lord.

7 "My holy name I will make known in the midst of My people Israel; and I will not let My holy name be profaned anymore. And the nations will know that I am the Lord, the Holy One in Israel. 8 Behold, it is coming and it shall be done," declares the Lord God. "That is the day of which I have spoken.

9 "Then those who inhabit the cities of Israel will go out and make fires with the weapons and burn them, both shields and bucklers, bows and arrows, war clubs and spears, and for seven years they will make fires of them. 10 They will not take wood from the field or gather firewood from the forests, for they will make fires with the weapons; and they will take the spoil of those who despoiled them and seize the plunder of those who plundered them," declares the Lord God.

Ezekiel
Ezekiel 39

11 "On that day I will give Gog a burial ground there in Israel, the valley of those who pass by east of the sea, and it will block off those who would pass by. So they will bury Gog there with all his horde, and they will call it the valley of Hamon-gog.

12 For seven months the house of Israel will be burying them in order to cleanse the land. 13 Even all the people of the land will bury them; and it will be to their renown on the day that I glorify Myself," declares the Lord God. 14 "They will set apart men who will constantly pass through the land, burying those who were passing through, even those left on the surface of the ground, in order to cleanse it. At the end of seven months they will make a search. 15 As those who pass through the land pass through and anyone sees a man's bone, then he will set up a marker by it until the buriers have buried it in the valley of Hamon-gog. 16 And even the name of the city will be Hamonah. So they will cleanse the land.'"

17 "As for you, son of man, thus says the Lord God, 'Speak to every kind of bird and to every beast of the field, "Assemble and come, gather from every side to My sacrifice which I am going to sacrifice for you, as a great sacrifice on the mountains of Israel, that you may eat flesh and drink blood. 18 You will eat the flesh of mighty men and drink the blood of the princes of the earth, as though they were rams, lambs, goats and bulls, all of them fatlings of Bashan. 19 So you will eat fat until you are glutted, and drink blood until you are drunk, from My sacrifice which I have sacrificed for you. 20 You will be glutted at My table with horses and charioteers, with mighty men and all the men of war," declares the Lord God.

21 "And I will set My glory among the nations; and all the nations will see My judgment which I have executed and My hand which I have laid on them. 22 And the house of Israel will know that I am the Lord their God from that day onward. 23 The nations will know that the house of Israel went into exile for their iniquity because they acted treacherously against Me, and I hid My face from them; so I gave them into the hand of their adversaries, and all of them fell by the sword. 24 According to their uncleanness and according to their transgressions I dealt with them, and I hid My face from them."'"

Israel Restored

25 Therefore thus says the Lord God, "Now I will restore the fortunes of Jacob and have mercy on the whole house of Israel; and I will be jealous for My holy name. 26 They will forget their disgrace and all their treachery which they perpetrated against Me, when they live securely on their own land with no one to make them afraid. 27 When I bring them back from the peoples and gather them from the lands of their enemies, then I shall be sanctified through them in the sight of the many nations. 28 Then they will know that I am the Lord their God because I made them go into exile among the nations, and then gathered them again to their own land; and I will leave none of them there any longer. 29 I will not hide My face from them any longer, for I will have poured out My Spirit on the house of Israel," declares the Lord God.

Ezekiel

Ezekiel 40

Vision of the Man with a Measuring Rod

40 In the twenty-fifth year of our exile, at the beginning of the year, on the tenth of the month, in the fourteenth year after the city was taken, on that same day the hand of the Lord was upon me and He brought me there. 2 In the visions of God He brought me into the land of Israel and set me on a very high mountain, and on it to the south there was a structure like a city. 3 So He brought me there; and behold, there was a man whose appearance was like the appearance of bronze, with a line of flax and a measuring rod in his hand; and he was standing in the gateway. 4 The man said to me, "Son of man, see with your eyes, hear with your ears, and give attention to all that I am going to show you; for you have been brought here in order to show it to you. Declare to the house of Israel all that you see."

Measurements Relating to the Temple

5 And behold, there was a wall on the outside of the temple all around, and in the man's hand was a measuring rod of six cubits, each of which was a cubit and a handbreadth. So he measured the thickness of the wall, one rod; and the height, one rod. 6 Then he went to the gate which faced east, went up its steps and measured the threshold of the gate, one rod in width; and the other threshold was one rod in width. 7 The guardroom was one rod long and one rod wide; and there were five cubits between the guardrooms. And the threshold of the gate by the porch of the gate facing inward was one rod. 8 Then he measured the porch of the gate facing inward, one rod. 9 He measured the porch of the gate, eight cubits; and its side pillars, two cubits. And the porch of the gate was faced inward.

10 The guardrooms of the gate toward the east numbered three on each side; the three of them had the same measurement. The side pillars also had the same measurement on each side.

11 And he measured the width of the gateway, ten cubits, and the length of the gate, thirteen cubits. 12 There was a barrier wall one cubit wide in front of the guardrooms on each side; and the guardrooms were six cubits square on each side. 13 He measured the gate from the roof of the one guardroom to the roof of the other, a width of twenty-five cubits from one door to the door opposite. 14 He made the side pillars sixty cubits high; the gate extended round about to the side pillar of the courtyard. 15 From the front of the entrance gate to the front of the inner porch of the gate was fifty cubits. 16 There were shuttered windows looking toward the guardrooms, and toward their side pillars within the gate all around, and likewise for the porches. And there were windows all around inside; and on each side pillar were palm tree ornaments.

17 Then he brought me into the outer court, and behold, there were chambers and a pavement made for the court all around; thirty chambers faced the pavement. 18 The pavement (that is, the lower pavement) was by the side of the gates, corresponding to the length of the gates. 19 Then he measured the width from the front of the lower gate to the front of the exterior of the inner court, a hundred cubits on the east and on the north.

20 As for the gate of the outer court which faced the north, he measured its length and its width. 21 It had three guardrooms on each side; and its side pillars and its porches had the same measurement as the first gate. Its length was fifty cubits and the width twenty-five cubits. 22 Its windows and its porches and its palm tree ornaments had the same measurements as the gate which faced toward the east; and it was reached by seven steps, and its porch was in front of them. 23 The inner court had a gate opposite the gate on the north as well as the gate on the east; and he measured a hundred cubits from gate to gate.

Ezekiel
Ezekiel 40

24 Then he led me toward the south, and behold, there was a gate toward the south; and he measured its side pillars and its porches according to those same measurements. 25 The gate and its porches had windows all around like those other windows; the length was fifty cubits and the width twenty-five cubits. 26 There were seven steps going up to it, and its porches were in front of them; and it had palm tree ornaments on its side pillars, one on each side. 27 The inner court had a gate toward the south; and he measured from gate to gate toward the south, a hundred cubits. 28 Then he brought me to the inner court by the south gate; and he measured the south gate according to those same measurements. 29 Its guardrooms also, its side pillars and its porches were according to those same measurements. And the gate and its porches had windows all around; it was fifty cubits long and twenty-five cubits wide. 30 There were porches all around, twenty-five cubits long and five cubits wide. 31 Its porches were toward the outer court; and palm tree ornaments were on its side pillars, and its stairway had eight steps.

32 He brought me into the inner court toward the east. And he measured the gate according to those same measurements. 33 Its guardrooms also, its side pillars and its porches were according to those same measurements. And the gate and its porches had windows all around; it was fifty cubits long and twenty-five cubits wide. 34 Its porches were toward the outer court; and palm tree ornaments were on its side pillars, on each side, and its stairway had eight steps.
35 Then he brought me to the north gate; and he measured it according to those same measurements, 36 with its guardrooms, its side pillars and its porches. And the gate had windows all around; the length was fifty cubits and the width twenty-five cubits. 37 Its side pillars were toward the outer court; and palm tree ornaments were on its side pillars on each side, and its stairway had eight steps.

38 A chamber with its doorway was by the side pillars at the gates; there they rinse the burnt offering. 39 In the porch of the gate were two tables on each side, on which to slaughter the burnt offering, the sin offering and the guilt offering. 40 On the outer side, as one went up to the gateway toward the north, were two tables; and on the other side of the porch of the gate were two tables. 41 Four tables were on each side next to the gate; or, eight tables on which they slaughter sacrifices. 42 For the burnt offering there were four tables of hewn stone, a cubit and a half long, a cubit and a half wide and one cubit high, on which they lay the instruments with which they slaughter the burnt offering and the sacrifice. 43 The double hooks, one handbreadth in length, were installed in the house all around; and on the tables was the flesh of the offering. 44 From the outside to the inner gate were chambers for the singers in the inner court, one of which was at the side of the north gate, with its front toward the south, and one at the side of the south gate facing toward the north. 45 He said to me, "This is the chamber which faces toward the south, intended for the priests who keep charge of the temple; 46 but the chamber which faces toward the north is for the priests who keep charge of the altar. These are the sons of Zadok, who from the sons of Levi come near to the Lord to minister to Him." 47 He measured the court, a perfect square, a hundred cubits long and a hundred cubits wide; and the altar was in front of the temple.

48 Then he brought me to the porch of the temple and measured each side pillar of the porch, five cubits on each side; and the width of the gate was three cubits on each side. 49 The length of the porch was twenty cubits and the width eleven cubits; and at the stairway by which it was ascended were columns belonging to the side pillars, one on each side.

Ezekiel

Ezekiel 43

Vision of the Glory of God Filling the Temple

43 Then he led me to the gate, the gate facing toward the east; 2 and behold, the glory of the God of Israel was coming from the way of the east. And His voice was like the sound of many waters; and the earth shone with His glory.

3 And it was like the appearance of the vision which I saw, like the vision which I saw when He came to destroy the city. And the visions were like the vision which I saw by the river Chebar; and I fell on my face. 4 And the glory of the Lord came into the house by the way of the gate facing toward the east. 5 And the Spirit lifted me up and brought me into the inner court; and behold, the glory of the Lord filled the house.

6 Then I heard one speaking to me from the house, while a man was standing beside me. 7 He said to me, "Son of man, this is the place of My throne and the place of the soles of My feet, where I will dwell among the sons of Israel forever. And the house of Israel will not again defile My holy name, neither they nor their kings, by their harlotry and by the corpses of their kings when they die, 8 by setting their threshold by My threshold and their door post beside My door post, with only the wall between Me and them. And they have defiled My holy name by their abominations which they have committed. So I have consumed them in My anger. 9 Now let them put away their harlotry and the corpses of their kings far from Me; and I will dwell among them forever.

10 "As for you, son of man, describe the temple to the house of Israel, that they may be ashamed of their iniquities; and let them measure the plan. 11 If they are ashamed of all that they have done, make known to them the design of the house, its structure, its exits, its entrances, all its designs, all its statutes, and all its laws. And write it in their sight, so that they may observe its whole design and all its statutes and do them. 12 This is the law of the house: its entire area on the top of the mountain all around shall be most holy. Behold, this is the law of the house.

The Altar of Sacrifice

13 "And these are the measurements of the altar by cubits (the cubit being a cubit and a handbreadth): the base shall be a cubit and the width a cubit, and its border on its edge round about one span; and this shall be the height of the base of the altar. 14 From the base on the ground to the lower ledge shall be two cubits and the width one cubit; and from the smaller ledge to the larger ledge shall be four cubits and the width one cubit. 15 The altar hearth shall be four cubits; and from the altar hearth shall extend upwards four horns. 16 Now the altar hearth shall be twelve cubits long by twelve wide, square in its four sides. 17 The ledge shall be fourteen cubits long by fourteen wide in its four sides, the border around it shall be half a cubit and its base shall be a cubit round about; and its steps shall face the east."

Ezekiel

Ezekiel 43

The Offerings

18 And He said to me, "Son of man, thus says the Lord God, 'These are the statutes for the altar on the day it is built, to offer burnt offerings on it and to sprinkle blood on it. 19 You shall give to the Levitical priests who are from the offspring of Zadok, who draw near to Me to minister to Me,' declares the Lord God, 'a young bull for a sin offering. 20 You shall take some of its blood and put it on its four horns and on the four corners of the ledge and on the border round about; thus you shall cleanse it and make atonement for it.

21 You shall also take the bull for the sin offering, and it shall be burned in the appointed place of the house, outside the sanctuary.

22 'On the second day you shall offer a male goat without blemish for a sin offering, and they shall cleanse the altar as they cleansed it with the bull.

23 When you have finished cleansing it, you shall present a young bull without blemish and a ram without blemish from the flock. 24 You shall present them before the Lord, and the priests shall throw salt on them, and they shall offer them up as a burnt offering to the Lord.

25 For seven days you shall prepare daily a goat for a sin offering; also a young bull and a ram from the flock, without blemish, shall be prepared.

26 For seven days they shall make atonement for the altar and purify it; so shall they consecrate it.

27 When they have completed the days, it shall be that on the eighth day and onward, the priests shall offer your burnt offerings on the altar, and your peace offerings; and I will accept you,' declares the Lord God."

Ezekiel

Ezekiel 44

Gate for the Prince

44 Then He brought me back by the way of the outer gate of the sanctuary, which faces the east; and it was shut. 2 The Lord said to me, "This gate shall be shut; it shall not be opened, and no one shall enter by it, for the Lord God of Israel has entered by it; therefore it shall be shut. 3 As for the prince, he shall sit in it as prince to eat bread before the Lord; he shall enter by way of the porch of the gate and shall go out by the same way."

4 Then He brought me by way of the north gate to the front of the house; and I looked, and behold, the glory of the Lord filled the house of the Lord, and I fell on my face. 5 The Lord said to me, "Son of man, mark well, see with your eyes and hear with your ears all that I say to you concerning all the statutes of the house of the Lord and concerning all its laws; and mark well the entrance of the house, with all exits of the sanctuary. 6 You shall say to the rebellious ones, to the house of Israel, 'Thus says the Lord God, "Enough of all your abominations, O house of Israel, 7 when you brought in foreigners, uncircumcised in heart and uncircumcised in flesh, to be in My sanctuary to profane it, even My house, when you offered My food, the fat and the blood; for they made My covenant void—this in addition to all your abominations. 8 And you have not kept charge of My holy things yourselves, but you have set foreigners to keep charge of My sanctuary."

9 'Thus says the Lord God, "No foreigner uncircumcised in heart and uncircumcised in flesh, of all the foreigners who are among the sons of Israel, shall enter My sanctuary. 10 But the Levites who went far from Me when Israel went astray, who went astray from Me after their idols, shall bear the punishment for their iniquity.

11 Yet they shall be ministers in My sanctuary, having oversight at the gates of the house and ministering in the house; they shall slaughter the burnt offering and the sacrifice for the people, and they shall stand before them to minister to them. 12 Because they ministered to them before their idols and became a stumbling block of iniquity to the house of Israel, therefore I have sworn against them," declares the Lord God, "that they shall bear the punishment for their iniquity. 13 And they shall not come near to Me to serve as a priest to Me, nor come near to any of My holy things, to the things that are most holy; but they will bear their shame and their abominations which they have committed. 14 Yet I will appoint them to keep charge of the house, of all its service and of all that shall be done in it.

Ezekiel

Ezekiel 44

Ordinances for the Levites

15 "But the Levitical priests, the sons of Zadok, who kept charge of My sanctuary when the sons of Israel went astray from Me, shall come near to Me to minister to Me; and they shall stand before Me to offer Me the fat and the blood," declares the Lord God. 16 "They shall enter My sanctuary; they shall come near to My table to minister to Me and keep My charge. 17 It shall be that when they enter at the gates of the inner court, they shall be clothed with linen garments; and wool shall not be on them while they are ministering in the gates of the inner court and in the house.

18 Linen turbans shall be on their heads and linen undergarments shall be on their loins; they shall not gird themselves with anything which makes them sweat.

19 When they go out into the outer court, into the outer court to the people, they shall put off their garments in which they have been ministering and lay them in the holy chambers; then they shall put on other garments so that they will not transmit holiness to the people with their garments.

20 Also they shall not shave their heads, yet they shall not let their locks grow long; they shall only trim the hair of their heads. 21 Nor shall any of the priests drink wine when they enter the inner court.

22 And they shall not marry a widow or a divorced woman but shall take virgins from the offspring of the house of Israel, or a widow who is the widow of a priest. 23 Moreover, they shall teach My people the difference between the holy and the profane, and cause them to discern between the unclean and the clean.

24 In a dispute they shall take their stand to judge; they shall judge it according to My ordinances. They shall also keep My laws and My statutes in all My appointed feasts and sanctify My sabbaths.

25 They shall not go to a dead person to defile themselves; however, for father, for mother, for son, for daughter, for brother, or for a sister who has not had a husband, they may defile themselves. 26 After he is cleansed, seven days shall elapse for him.

27 On the day that he goes into the sanctuary, into the inner court to minister in the sanctuary, he shall offer his sin offering," declares the Lord God.

Revelation

Revelation 21

The New Heaven and Earth

21 Then I saw a new heaven and a new earth; for the first heaven and the first earth passed away, and there is no longer any sea.

2 And I saw the holy city, new Jerusalem, coming down out of heaven from God, made ready as a bride adorned for her husband.

3 And I heard a loud voice from the throne, saying, "Behold, the tabernacle of God is among men, and He will dwell among them, and they shall be His people, and God Himself will be among them,

4 and He will wipe away every tear from their eyes; and there will no longer be any death; there will no longer be any mourning, or crying, or pain; the first things have passed away."

5 And He who sits on the throne said, "Behold, I am making all things new." And He said, "Write, for these words are faithful and true."

6 Then He said to me, "It is done. I am the Alpha and the Omega, the beginning and the end. I will give to the one who thirsts from the spring of the water of life without cost.

7 He who overcomes will inherit these things, and I will be his God and he will be My son. 8 But for the cowardly and unbelieving and abominable and murderers and immoral persons and sorcerers and idolaters and all liars, their part will be in the lake that burns with fire and brimstone, which is the second death."

9 Then one of the seven angels who had the seven bowls full of the seven last plagues came and spoke with me, saying, "Come here, I will show you the bride, the wife of the Lamb."

Revelation

Revelation 21

The New Jerusalem

10 And he carried me away in the Spirit to a great and high mountain, and showed me the holy city, Jerusalem, coming down out of heaven from God, 11 having the glory of God. Her brilliance was like a very costly stone, as a stone of crystal-clear jasper.

12 It had a great and high wall, with twelve gates, and at the gates twelve angels; and names were written on them, which are the names of the twelve tribes of the sons of Israel. 13 There were three gates on the east and three gates on the north and three gates on the south and three gates on the west. 14 And the wall of the city had twelve foundation stones, and on them were the twelve names of the twelve apostles of the Lamb.

15 The one who spoke with me had a gold measuring rod to measure the city, and its gates and its wall. 16 The city is laid out as a square, and its length is as great as the width; and he measured the city with the rod, fifteen hundred miles; its length and width and height are equal.

17 And he measured its wall, seventy-two yards, according to human measurements, which are also angelic measurements. 18 The material of the wall was jasper; and the city was pure gold, like clear glass.

19 The foundation stones of the city wall were adorned with every kind of precious stone. The first foundation stone was jasper; the second, sapphire; the third, chalcedony; the fourth, emerald; 20 the fifth, sardonyx; the sixth, sardius; the seventh, chrysolite; the eighth, beryl; the ninth, topaz; the tenth, chrysoprase; the eleventh, jacinth; the twelfth, amethyst.

21 And the twelve gates were twelve pearls; each one of the gates was a single pearl. And the street of the city was pure gold, like transparent glass.

22 I saw no temple in it, for the Lord God the Almighty and the Lamb are its temple. 23 And the city has no need of the sun or of the moon to shine on it, for the glory of God has illumined it, and its lamp is the Lamb.

24 The nations will walk by its light, and the kings of the earth will bring their glory into it.

25 In the daytime (for there will be no night there) its gates will never be closed; 26 and they will bring the glory and the honor of the nations into it; 27 and nothing unclean, and no one who practices abomination and lying, shall ever come into it, but only those whose names are written in the Lamb's book of life.

Revelation

Revelation 22

Revelation 22New American Standard Bible
(NASB)
The River and the Tree of Life
22 Then he showed me a river of the water of
life, clear as crystal, coming from the throne of
God and of the Lamb, 2 in the middle of its
street. On either side of the river was the tree of
life, bearing twelve kinds of fruit, yielding its fruit
every month; and the leaves of the tree were for
the healing of the nations. 3 There will no longer
be any curse; and the throne of God and of the
Lamb will be in it, and His bond-servants will
serve Him; 4 they will see His face, and His name
will be on their foreheads. 5 And there will no
longer be any night; and they will not have need
of the light of a lamp nor the light of the sun,
because the Lord God will illumine them; and
they will reign forever and ever.
6 And he said to me, "These words are faithful
and true"; and the Lord, the God of the spirits of
the prophets, sent His angel to show to His
bond-servants the things which must soon take
place.
7 "And behold, I am coming quickly. Blessed is he
who heeds the words of the prophecy of this
book."

How will it all end?
What is the culmination of God's mission on earth?
Revelation 7:9–10, NASB

After these things I looked, and behold, a great multitude which no one could count, from every nation and *all* tribes and peoples and tongues, standing before the throne and before the Lamb, clothed in white robes, and palm branches *were* in their hands;

10 and they cry out with a loud voice, saying, "Salvation to our God who sits on the throne, and to the Lamb."

Observation and Reflection

Summative assessment
Position paper notes

What I believe:

Why do I believe it?

What difference will it make in my life?

Applied Theology

Doctrine & Apologetics

INVITED TO GO AND TEACH

Unit Essential Questions

1. Is the Christian experience valid?

2. How does Christianity differ from other world religions?

3. What is worship, and how has my worship changed as a result of this course?

Reading

Know Why You Believe, Chapters 11-12

Unit Learning Assessments

Summative:

Position paper

Daily Learning Plan

12.1 Is the Christian experience valid?

12.2 How does Christianity differ from other world religions?

12.3 What is my next step, and how do I reproduce what I've learned?

12.4 Final questions

Applied theology scenarios

After leaving school, you start attending college and begin the process of looking for churches.

One of the first churches you begin to attend seems like it would be a good fit. The people are nice, the worship is great, and the pastor seems like a cool guy.

You begin talking with some of the people and asking questions about the church, and it casually slips out that the church believes the Bible "contains the Word of God."

- Is that a problem?

- Why or why not?

- Back up your response with Scripture.

Read Matthew 28:11-15. According to this passage, even the enemies of Christ admitted His tomb was empty. The truth of Christ's resurrection rests on how the tomb was emptied. The authorities claimed Jesus' followers removed the body. Other explanations are often given, as well: that the authorities moved the body or the disciples returned to the wrong tomb.

- What makes these explanations reasonable or unreasonable? Back up your position.

- Give nine "proofs" of the resurrection of Christ: three from Scripture, three historical (non-Christian), and three circumstantial.

Your friend at work is a Jehovah's Witness. One day, while you are talking over lunch, he explains to you his belief that Jesus never actually claimed to be God. In fact, he pulls out his version of the Bible and shows you that in John 1, his Bible says Jesus was simply "a" god.

1. What is your response?

2. What argument would you use from the text to show how and why his version is a blatant mistranslation of Scripture?

3. What verses would you reference to show how Christ claimed to be God in a way that even His enemies clearly understood His claim?

Two nice young men come to your door. They are both wearing white shirts, black pants, and ties. You see their bicycles parked alongside the curb. Their nametags say their names are Elder Smith and Elder Jones. They would like to come in and "do a Bible study" with you.

a. Under what circumstances would you invite them in?

b. What items of spiritual warfare should you be particularly aware of?

c. What ground rules should you set as a result?

d. Outline their doctrinal position regarding the nature of Christ.

e. What Scripture would you use as your apologetic to their claims?

Is Christianity rational?

notes

"Jesus replied: 'Love the Lord your God with all your heart and with all your soul and with all your mind.'"

- Matthew 22:37, NIV

Premise: God expects us to believe in Him based on:

1. Comprehensible evidence

2. Intellectual engagement

3. Logical reasoning

However:

"The pull of moralism disguised as an intellectual problem can be seemingly strong, but often it is simply a smoke screen that is covering moral rebellion."

- Paul Little

"We cannot pander to a man's intellectual arrogance, but we must cater to his intellectual integrity."

- John Stott

Applied Theology
Reading notes

Know Why You Believe, Chapter 11: Does Christianity differ from other world religions?

1. Many people believe all religions worship the same God but call that God by different names. Consider Buddhism, Hinduism, Islam, and Christianity (pp. 150-156).

Know Why You Believe, Chapter 12: Is the Christian experience valid?

How would you effectively answer a person who thinks your Christian experience is a fantasy? (1 Peter 3:15)

2. Summarize the chief points of each religion, including the religion's ultimate goal, method of achieving that goal, and concept of a deity.

Summative assessment
Position paper notes

What I believe:

Why do I believe it?

What difference will it make in my life?

Mid-term reflection

Name: _____ Period: _____

Reflection on the first half of class

1. What has God been teaching me?

2. What have I learned through this process?

3. What is one surprise I've had?

4. What is one thing that stands out to me when I think about growth in my life?

5. What is one area where I would like to see more growth between now and the end of the semester?

6. How do you feel about where you are in the class right now?

   My grade:

   My level of learning:

   My position papers:

7. One question I still need answered between now and the end of the semester is.

Final reflection

First Name: _____ Last Name: _____ Period: _____

Reflection on the class

1. How did you feel when you started this project?

2. How do you feel now that you have finished?

3. What changed?

4. At what point did change happen or begin to start?

5. What stands out? What was a highlight of this experience for you?

6. What have you learned from this experience?

    1. About yourself

    2. About God

7. What grade would you give yourself for this project? Why?